The 24 Hour Currency

The 24 Hour Curren¢y

5 Principles to Revolutionize your Relationship with Time

JENNIFER F. ARTHUR

The 24 Hour Currency - 5 Principles to Revolutionize Your Relationship with Time

Cloud Cover Press, LLC

FIRST EDITION: November 2025

For Worldwide Distribution
ISBN: 979-8-9931748-0-8

Front cover design: Jennifer F. Arthur & Dorretha Bennem
Back cover & spine design: Olyaemi Bolaji

Cloud Cover Press books may be purchased in bulk for business, educational or promotional use. For information please contact your local bookseller or Cloud Cover Press directly at info@cloudcoverpress.com

CONTENTS

PRINCIPLE #4: GUARDING YOUR TIME

PRINCIPLE #5: USING YOUR TIME AS CURRENCY

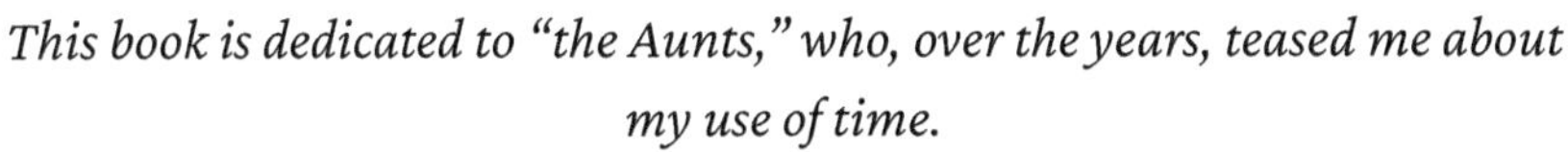

This book is dedicated to "the Aunts," who, over the years, teased me about my use of time.

Thank you for loving me, and laughing with me!

I HAVE ONLY JUST A MINUTE

I have only just a minute,
only sixty seconds in it.
Forced upon me, can't refuse it.
Didn't seek it, didn't choose it.
But it's up to me
to use it.
I must suffer if I lose it.
Give account if I abuse it.
Just a tiny little minute,
but eternity is in it.

~Dr. Benjamin E. Mays

INTRODUCTION

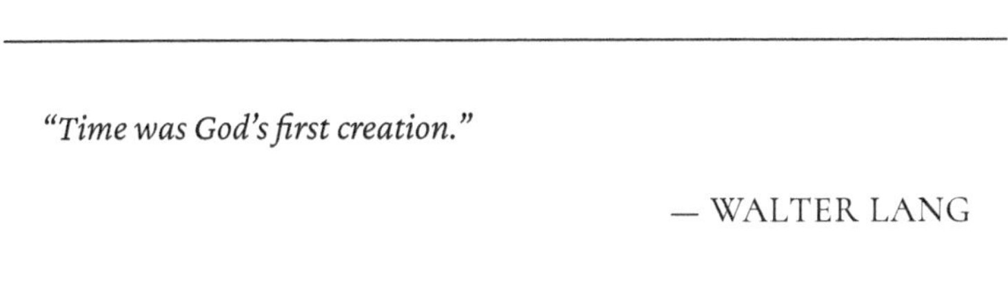

It's go time, time for some action, take your time, what time is it, I don't have time, I don't want to waste my time, time is ticking, ticking time bomb. All sayings we've heard or said with relation to time. Why are we, as humans, so fixated on time? I believe it's because we know our time here is finite. If we had an infinite amount of it, it would be a non-issue. Much like choosing how we spend our money, choosing how we spend our time is of equal concern. Time is all around us; we are affected by the time of day, the time we need to be somewhere, the time it takes to complete a task, the time of the month, the time of the year, and on it goes.

If you had an infinite amount of time, what would you do with it? What legacy do you want to leave behind in this world? What are your dreams, hopes, and ambitions? The vast majority of us in the

Western World believe we only have one life to live. If we believe this, then why do so many of us live as if we have all the time in the world? Why do we dream small? Why do we live small? Why do we put our dreams on the shelf for the "right" time? I know so many people who have died before the age of 50. We are not guaranteed the next day, the next week, the next month, or the next year.

Take the course, make the move, leave the job, pursue the opportunity, take the trip, start the business or whatever other thing that feels like a risk for you. Essentially, if you have something that you want to live for, do it NOW!

If you are reading this book, you may often feel like a hamster on a wheel, a rat trying to find that proverbial cheese. Hustling and grinding, but never really getting ahead. You may find the demands of your friends and family often taking precedence over your goals and desires. Pulled in a million different directions, and feeling like time is not your own. You may be in a job or career that you hate. Quite possibly, you feel like there is not enough time in a day, week, month, or year. You may find yourself wondering about what it is you are supposed to be doing here on this planet, and how you are supposed to be using your time. You look up year after year, and very few of your goals have been achieved.

What's the difference between highly accomplished people and the rest of us? Do they have more time? Of course not. We all have the same 24 hours in a day; it is what we do with it that makes the difference. One thing that rings true about successful, accomplished people is that they have taken the time to focus on what is most important to them, and their priorities are often in line with what they value most.

Time impacts everything we do on Earth. At the end of the day, it is essentially YOUR time, and you get to choose exactly what you will do with it. Will you spend it working, with friends, traveling, or pursuing your dreams?

While none of us is guaranteed how long we live, as long as we are alive, we are all allotted the same 24 hours per day. It is the great equalizer. If time were a currency, we'd all be wealthy. If time were a political ideology, we'd be a socialist society. If time were a diversity issue, we'd be a homogeneous culture. You get the picture. Yet, it is how we spend each 24 hours that determines how productive, accomplished, or fulfilled we are. It is the aggregate of the 24 hours that we stitch together over the course of days, weeks, months, and years that make up the sum total of our lives. It is within this 24-hour time span that we plant and water the seeds of dreams, spend time with loved ones, create memories, start businesses, and those same 24 hours that we rest, recuperate, regroup, and relish in all that life has to offer.

Perhaps you know the lyrics to the classic song by the Byrds, *Turn! Turn! Turn! (To Everything there is a Season)* - "A time to be born, a time to die, a time to plant, a time to reap, a time to kill, a time to heal, a time to laugh, a time to weep, a time to build up, a time to break down, a time to dance, a time to mourn, a time of love, a time of hate, a time of war, a time of peace, a time to gain, a time to lose, a time to rend, a time to sow." If you know this song, you may also know it was borrowed from the words of King Solomon recorded in the book of Ecclesiastes, in the Old Testament Bible. Solomon was also documented as being one of the wisest people to have ever lived. So wise in fact that he made a fortune because people traveled far and wide, offering him gifts in exchange for his council - think the multi-billion dollar coaching industry. Solomon acquired orchards, homes, vineyards, and wealth galore. Still, one of his major contributions outside of the books of Proverbs, Ecclesiastes, and Song of Songs was his understanding that there is a time for everything. What is most crucial to the human experience is that time is finite.

Time, unlike money, can never be recovered. When we fully grasp how short life is and that each day is not promised, then we will be much more mindful of how we spend our days. When we know our values, what is most important to us, our "Why", we will start to change the way we approach time. When we grasp how finite we are, we will become empowered to cease doing work we loathe, and pursue the things in life that light our soul on fire, the things we were meant to do. Once we identify this, we can then utilize our time in a purposeful way.

In this book, we will dive deeply into five time principles, designed to guide you to the path of becoming an excellent steward of your time, with the goal of living a life of purpose and meaning.

You will learn how you personally relate to time and find ways in which you can more efficiently utilize your time. We will look at time from many different perspectives, learning how to leverage it, manage it, juggle it, savor, and appreciate it.

This book has both practical applications of time management and planning tactics, coupled with theoretical, philosophical, existential, and spiritual conversations about time. While this is not a religious book, there will be moments when a scripture or two is referenced for its relevance to a topic of discussion.

While I have developed a system for managing time that has been highly effective for me, which I will share, that is not the sole emphasis of this book. Whether you use my system or find another, the idea is that you find or create a system that works best for you so that you can create your desired life.

WHAT INSPIRED THIS BOOK?

Since I can remember, I have been keenly aware of time. When I was eight years old, I reasoned with myself that if I did my school work as soon as I got home, then I'd have more time to play outside with my friends, without unfinished homework looming over me. Over the years, I have continued to cultivate an acute awareness of how I spend my time, and the concurrent fascination with the fact that it is a key factor of our very existence.

In my second year of college, I purchased my first day planner because without it, it was impossible to juggle my classes, assignments, projects, and upcoming tests, in addition to keeping a part-time job, and being heavily involved in my campus ministry.

After graduation, I faced new time challenges and restraints. How was I to manage the world of work, keeping in shape, participating in church activities, spending time with friends and family, making time for travel, and romantic relationships, not to mention discerning between which new project I wanted to focus on? The planner never left my side.

As a young adult, I became deeply aware of how finite life was, and that if I was going to accomplish what had been put on my heart at 14, to be an entrepreneur, and at the age of 18, a philanthropist, I'd have to get a hold of my time.

The term “You're doing too much,” has often plagued me. Whether it was coming from the words of another or my own insecurities. My aunts used to taunt me, saying if you want to get together with Jennifer, you need to schedule it between 1:25 p.m. and 1:47 p.m., poking at how busy my schedule was. Fast forward to decades later, it was these same aunts who asked, upon the heels of publishing my first novel, “Jennifer, how is it that you get so much done?” Initially, I was not sure how to answer the question, until one day, lying on my bed, in quiet reflection, it came to me. I get so much done because I am good with my time, and thus the birth of this book.

Over the years, not only have I been able to effectively handle my personal projects, but I've also successfully managed my time in various professional roles. In my last nine-to-five role, I was the head of a department at a rapidly growing graduate program in the high-volume, fast-paced admissions office. I managed a constant revolving door of anywhere between seven and twelve projects at one time, during the course of my five years there. My responsibilities included overseeing the entire recruitment process, which involved planning our attendance at nearly 60 national graduate fairs per year, including shipping items, traveling, and more. In addition, I planned events that ranged from 20 to 500-plus attendees at both the main campus and our three satellite locations. Another function of the multifaceted role was planning and conducting on and off-campus information sessions for prospective students, reviewing applications, and giving feedback to denied students. I oversaw the scheduling process of the hour-long, in-person inquiry meetings with prospective students with whom I met. I was responsible for our email marketing plan, including creating and sending the emails. I supervised a team of staff, including student workers, a full-time recruitment coordinator who ran point at our satellite campuses, and a board of 8-10 student ambassadors. I planned our yearly recruitment retreat and volunteer thank-you lunch, and oversaw the creation of several promotional videos. Under my care was also an inbound inquiry email account, and more. I'm exhausted just thinking about it! I would not have been able to accomplish any of this without proper planning and effective time management.

During the process of writing this book I worked several (temporary) full time jobs, ran a small business, wrote and packaged three screenplays, marketed my novel, *Souls by the Sea*, consulted several small business clients, decorated multiple homes, started another book, this not even mentioning my personal life. Again, the planner was always by my side.

Having known I'd be an entrepreneur since I was 14 years old, I looked at my work life as a training ground of sorts. After earning my masters in Social Work - a move toward philanthropy - I worked several jobs that benefited high-risk youth, and over the years, I have pursued a number of entrepreneurial endeavors, in between desk jobs. It wasn't until I was in my mid-40s, while in a job I loathed, that I made the declaration that I wanted only to use the creative part of myself to make my living. It was around this time that I started receiving more interior design clients, and a couple of years prior, I started writing screenplays, a new form of writing for me. While I had been writing for years (poetry, grants for nonprofits, and fiction), it wasn't until the last few years that I actually discovered my *love* of writing, and it was then that I knew I wanted to do this for the rest of my life.

In the midst of writing this book, I read a book called *Waking the Dead* by John Eldredge. At one point, the author asked God who he thought he was, and God told him he was his Wallace, from Braveheart. I decided to do the same. I asked God, "Who am I?" The name Dorothy popped into my head. I laughed. Dorothy from the Wizard of Oz? Why her? Through the process, I realized that, like me, Dorothy was a dreamer, and she also helped those in her life to discover and pursue their dreams. This revelation did not shock me, but rather confirmed what I had known about myself for many years. I have always been a dreamer and have actively pursued the things of my heart, whether big or small. With the same passion I pursue my own dreams, I have that same drive to help others do the same.

My hope for you is that you don't have to wait until your 40s to find your passion and pursue your dreams. However, if you are in your 40s or beyond, I want to spur you to utilize the remaining time you have to find and do what you love.

Additionally, I hope this book will help you identify your time pitfalls, time sucks, time deficits, and turn them into gold mines of time in order for you to relish your life, identify areas for growth, take back control of your time, and to ultimately create the life you have always dreamt of.

WHO IS THIS BOOK FOR?

Whatever type of professional you are, you know that time is of the utmost importance when trying to meet deadlines at work, juggling work and a family, and building a business. This book is for the young professional leader who is just starting out, the professional who has been in the work world for some time or the professional who is burnt out on work and wants to start their own entrepreneurial endeavors. This book is also for individuals seeking to discover their dreams or find time to pursue them in today's busy world.

Whether you're a planner, a non-planner, someone longing to grasp how to maximize your time, a person struggling to meet goals, someone who is excellent at meeting goals, and needs some new tips, an individual who enjoys looking at life from a philosophical and existential stance, a solopreneur, entrepreneur, mommypreneur, influencer, or nine-to-fiver, you are in the right place. If you are a dreamer, a doer, live life by the seat of your pantser, the person who pays little attention to time, and someone who can think of nothing but time, there is something here for you.

Whether you believe you only have one life to live or that you will be back for a re-do, you still have a choice of how you will spend your time. My hope is that you are inspired to use the relatively small amount of time you have here to be your best self, live your dreams, do the things you were meant to do, or deliver the important message only you can. All time, past, present, and future are crucial parts of determining who you are and who you will become.

PRINCIPLE #1: UNDERSTANDING YOUR PERSONAL RELATIONSHIP WITH TIME

"Time does not change us. It unfolds us."

— MAX FRISCH

Many people believe that time is a human construct. In actuality, nature is the originator of time. It takes a full 24 hours for the earth to revolve on its axis, rotating in a way that creates day and night. There are four, three-month cycles that create the seasons. Even the moon has its cycle, affecting the tides. Nature also dictates the time functions of our bodies - how much rest we need each night, the most optimal time of month for a woman to conceive, and the length of time our bodies need to recover from injury.

It is humans, however, who have determined how we *interact* with time. We decide what types of food we eat depending on the time of day, and what time of year to take vacations. It is humankind that has created the school year and the work week. While some of these constructs have been in place for so long and are seemingly impossible to escape, as individuals, we decide our relationship with the time that has been given to us. We get to decide when we play, when we rest, and when we just get to *be*. Some rise with the sun, and others flourish in the night. Spontaneity is the way of one person, while planning is essential for another. Each person has a different relationship with time, and how each person uses their 24-hour currency may look starkly different from the next.

In the following pages, we will examine the spectrums and patterns of how we relate to and interact with time. We will uncover a variety of concepts, ideals, and realities that all affect our personal relationship with time. I invite you to reflect on yourself, your habits, and how you personally interact with time, considering your uniqueness.

1

OUR PERSONAL RELATIONSHIP WITH TIME

"Know thyself."

— SOCRATES & OTHER GREEK PHILOSOPHERS

Are you a procrastinator? Do you feel like you waste time? Do you take longer than some to complete projects? The only way to truly and successfully move through life is to be honest with ourselves so that we can make the proper adjustments. At the very least, we need to be aware of the truth of who we are - the good, the bad, and the ugly. We all have strengths and we all have flaws. Both need to be acknowledged in order to be a whole human. Later, in this book, I will share my greatest weakness (as it relates to time). For now, I'll share my strengths. I would consider myself a time connoisseur. I am an energizer bunny when it comes to 'doing', and my time is truly my most valuable currency. There is very little that I would consider a haphazard use of my time. In everything I do, I make my best effort to move forward with purpose, always with time considerations in the back of my mind. Sure, there are times when I just veg out, binge-watch a riveting show, chill with friends, or lie listlessly on my bed, but for the most part, I'm hyper-aware of how I spend my time. When I used to work a nine-to-five job, and was offered the choice between more vacation time or more money, I would struggle with the decision, but in the end, more time would generally win. How do you like to spend your time? What are your strengths and deficits when it comes to how you use your time? How would you like to shift how you use your time?

OUR PERSONAL PACE

In job interviews, I used to ask candidates where they saw themselves with respect to their work style. Were they a tortoise or a hare? There was no right or wrong answer, simply a way to understand how people function when it comes to their process for getting things done.

According to an article in *Psychology Today,* there are two main styles of working, like in Aessop's fable, *The Tortoise and the Hare.* The tortoise was slow and steady, and the hare was swift and intense. The tortoise is fine with working everyday, but for shorter periods of time, (i.e. seven days a week for three hours per day) slowly and steadily completing the work, whereas the hare would prefer to work fewer days, but for longer hours, in order to get larger chunks done in a shorter amount of time, with sprints and bursts of effort (i.e. three days per week for seven hours per day). I used to think I was a hare, because I do things quickly, but have discovered of late that I am much more of a tortoise when it comes to working. However, nothing is simply black or white, and many things fall on a continuum. Where do you see yourself with respect to your work pace? Are you a tortoise or a hare?

THERE'S A REASON FOR THE SEASONS

Have you ever heard someone refer to themselves as a summer or winter? They are generally stating what type of mood their personality is. Summers are people who are generally cheerful, see things from a positive perspective, and are upbeat. Winters are typically a bit more on the melancholy side, pensive, thinkers, and philosophers. I recently learned that seasons even have significance for the types of colors we wear. Spring and summer look best in pastels and softer colors, while winters rock the jewel tones, and autumns look good in colors that remind us of the changing seasons.

In general, seasons affect our mood no matter our personality type. For instance, spring is a time of rebirth, reinventing yourself, and purging items in your home. The spring season offers the promise of renewal that is much needed after a long, cold winter. If spring is your favorite season, you are likely someone who desires new experiences.

Summer is a time to play, relax, and unwind. If summer is your favorite time of year, it might mean that you love getting out and living an active lifestyle. The warm months of summer are a time to travel and enjoy the outdoors. You probably tend to be outgoing, and people would likely describe you as upbeat, personable, and assertive.

Autumn is a time for slowing down, harvesting, collecting, and building up your storehouse to prepare for winter. Much like spring, fall can also be a time for a fresh start, and the vibrant, warm colors and cooler weather of autumn appeal to your constant desire for change. The upcoming holidays may inspire you to reflect back on the past year and make plans for the upcoming year.

Winter is a time for hibernation, rest, being still, and spending time indoors. If you count the chilly months of winter as your favorite season of all, it probably means that you tend to be a bit of a homebody. Unveiling your sweater collection and curling up on the couch with a cup of cocoa might sound like an ideal afternoon.

I am an autumn and a spring person, mostly for the reasons that I love change, renewal and growth. Isn't it interesting how one person can be invigorated by the cold, and another can feel paralyzed by it? I feel like I want to crawl into a ball when it is too hot out, but give me 65-degree weather with a sky full of storm clouds, and I feel on top of the world. Yet some people feel completely revitalized by the heat. For me, it would be foolish to go outside and exercise in the middle of a hot day because it is not an ideal time for my body. Knowing and understanding the season that resonates most with you may help you determine when you are at your optimal. This is likely the time when you decide to take a trip, take on a new project, or tackle a new challenge.

PRIME TIME

Want to binge-watch Netflix or spend an hour scrolling through Facebook? No problem, but try to avoid using your prime time hours —the time in your day when you're most optimally effective —and instead use your downtime, that time when your brain or body is shutting down and you can literally do nothing more except zone out.

Prime time is the period when you are at your best, with the most energy for the task at hand. It is during this time that you will want to tackle your most challenging mental and physical tasks, which may include passion projects.

Your prime time might vary depending on the type of task. For instance, I tend to be my best physically in the morning. It is during this time that I do things like house chores, running errands, DIY projects, rearranging furniture, organizing, and exercising. In the evenings, my mind is more settled, and I find that I can best focus on mental tasks such as strategizing for projects, trying new recipes, researching, finding home remedies, writing, making important phone calls, reading through paperwork, and planning.

Prime time is different for everyone. If you're unsure of your prime time, consider asking yourself this essential question. Do you tend to be sluggish or full of energy during a particular time of day?

Do you find yourself up until all hours of the night? Or maybe your eyes become droopy once it's dark out. Whatever the case, the science behind this is called our chronotype. A person's chronotype is the propensity for the individual to sleep or be awake at a particular time during a 24-hour period. Most people are either a morning (lark) or a night (owl). Chances are, you already know whether you're a morning person or a night person. Recent studies have added afternoon people to the mix. While there may be schools of thought around one being better than the other, there is simply no real proof of this. In a study posted by *Fast Company*, the data showed some upsides and downsides of each.

Night Owls are most alert at night, and typically turn in long after dark. This is me, all the way! When I was in grad school, I used to start writing papers at 10:00 p.m., then head to bed around midnight. To this day, I have to force myself to be in bed by midnight, otherwise I could easily be up until 2:00 a.m. on a regular basis. Is this you? Do you feel most alive at night, when the world has settled down, the kids are in bed, and the business of the day has waned? Can you connect best during this time, think the best, create the most? In my poetry writing days, I wrote a poem called *The Sound of Midnight* because I thought this time of day was so magical.

Owls tend to be more adventuresome, creative, and inclined to seek new experiences. They are also known to do better when it comes to memory, cognitive ability, and processing speed. One study showed they may even be richer. On the flip side, those linked to this chronotype have a propensity to drink and smoke more.

Larks are known for being up with the sun and tend to hit the sack at a respectable evening hour. They often feel accomplished when they have gotten many things done long before the hustle and bustle of the day. Terms like early to bed, early to rise, and the early bird gets the worm apply. Is this you? My stepfather has been a surfer for most of his life, and for a surfer, it is an up before dawn kind of party. As a kid, I was bundled up, on the sand, with snacks in hand, before sunrise. We left the beach right around noon, just as the "regular" beach dwellers, laden with their coolers and beach umbrellas, were making their way to the sand.

Larks may tend to be happier as a whole, procrastinate less, and are often very cooperative, proactive, and agreeable. However, they are less likely to be risk-takers.

If you don't quite fit in among the morning people or night owls, well, you might soon have your own, more relatable, sleep category.

Researchers propose two more chronotypes: the "afternoon" person and the "napper." Of all the chronotypes, afternoon people wake up the sleepiest and then they become alert around 11 a.m., staying that way until about 5 p.m., after which they get tired again. The "nappers" wake up alert and stay alert until about 11 a.m., after which they get really tired until about 3 p.m. After 3 p.m. until about 10 p.m., they are alert and productive again, as was first reported by *Psychology Today*.

These labels are less definitive, but rather people fall on some part of a spectrum, and these chronotypes can shift over a person's lifetime.

HARRIED, STRESSED & UNDER DURESS

How we show up to life is completely within our control. No one can *make* you mad, *make* you sad, or *make* you...fill in the blank. We get to choose our responses. How do you choose to go through life? Are you constantly stressed and harried, or do you take life with a stride? Each option is available to you, but only one is beneficial.

You can see this play out on the road. Are you the person foaming at the mouth to rush to a red light? If so, what will those two to three seconds it takes to frantically swing in front of that car you feel is moving too slowly really going to do for you? If you're running late, you are already late. The fact is we are all in a rush at some point or another, but we still get to choose how we show up, even under these circumstances.

Stress comes in many forms, and driving is just a small example. We experience stress at home, at work, and in our everyday ordinary lives. It all depends on how you want to go through life. Do you want to show up distressed and on edge, or peaceful and calm? The choice is yours.

2
LIVING ON PURPOSE

"True happiness is not attained through self-gratification, but through fidelity to a worthy purpose."

— HELEN KELLER

IF TIME COULD STAND STILL

Some of us don't take strides toward our goals because we are afraid of how we will be perceived. What if you could live your dreams without inhibitions or limitations, care of money or criticism from others? How would your life look if you believed you were not being watched? The reality is that most people are scarcely looking at or thinking about you, they are far too busy focusing on themselves, and worrying about what others are thinking of them. One of my favorite comedians, Chris Delia, in one of his stand up shows said "Our lives are like a movie, we are the star, and everyone else is just in the background." With that in mind, how would you craft your life if the fear of judgment was removed? What kinds of decisions would you make? It is sometimes difficult to block out the chatter of friends, family, and society when it comes to pursuing that which is deep in our hearts - the unceasing call of our dreams. If we lived like no one was watching, perhaps we could be our most authentic selves and unabashedly follow the path for which we were called.

TURNING BACK THE HANDS OF TIME

There have been so many movies and books relating to time travel, *The Time Traveler's Wife, Outlander, Time Bandits, Back to the Future* to name a few well-knowns. Why is time travel so fascinating to us? I believe one of the most powerful superpowers would be to have the ability to rewind time. What would you change if you had your very own time machine? Would you fix a relationship, take back something you said in an argument, or say yes to that opportunity? Choose a different place to live, tell the love interest the truth about how you felt? The one reality that is constant in the human experience is that once time has passed, there is no getting it back.

A regret is defined as a feeling of sorrow or remorse for a fault, act, loss, or disappointment. In simpler terms, the things in life we wish we would have done or not done. Regrets come from not trying; failures come when you do. I believe wholeheartedly that it is better to have a basket full of failures than a treasure chest filled with regrets.

I have made it my life goal to ensure I don't die filled with regret, and because of this, I do my best to pursue all of my heart's desires, which includes things big and small. Big endeavors may include traveling, pursuing a romantic relationship, or attending an event that will propel your business forward. Smaller things might be saying what is on your mind, in the moment. Far too many people live with regrets, and many people, on their deathbed, could easily say, "I wish," fill in the blank. According to *Forbes*, the following are the 25 most regrettable moments:

1. Working so much at the expense of family and friends
2. Not standing up to bullies in school and in life
3. Not having stayed in touch with good friends from youth
4. Not turning off my phone more/should have left my phone at home
5. Breaking up with my true love
6. Worrying about what others thought about me too much
7. Not having enough self-confidence
8. Living the life that my parents wanted me to live, instead of the one I wanted to
9. Not applying for that "dream job"
10. Wish I would have been happier more and taken life less seriously
11. Wish I would have gone on more trips with family and friends
12. Letting my marriage break down
13. Should have taught my kids to do more stuff
14. Wish I would have buried the hatchet with a family member or old friend
15. Not trusting the voice in the back of my head more
16. Not asking that girl/boy out
17. Getting involved with the wrong group of friends when I was younger
18. Not getting that degree (high school or college)
19. Choosing the practical job over the one I really wanted
20. Not spending more time with my kids
21. Not taking care of my health when I had the chance
22. Not having the courage to get up and talk at the funeral or an important event

23. Not visiting a dying friend
24. Not learning another language
25. Wishing I'd been a better mother/father

Do any of the above listed regrets resonate with you? Maybe none of them are things you can relate to or have yet to experience. In that case, good! Hopefully, they bring an awareness to your future decision-making self, to ensure that none of them ever end up on your list.

THE EVER ENDURING QUESTION

Human beings are on a quest, a lifelong path of discovery to find the answer to an ever enduring question... "What is my purpose?" According to Dictionary.com the definition of purpose is the reason for which something exists or is done, made, or used.

With this definition in mind the (quest)ion we are ultimately seeking is, "Why do I exist?" For many, a career path is often tied to purpose because this is one of the most powerful expressions that often combines our passions, talents, abilities, and gifts (a deeper dive into this in Chapter 4). While it is not always the case that we make a living utilizing these expressions, these components of ourselves are frequently tied to the activities we devote much of our time to.

Looking more deeply, our purpose, which indeed is commonly tied to our natural gifts and talents, is not solely for our own personal enjoyment, but rather to be shared with those we encounter, and inherently for the greater good of humanity. Imagine if the inventors of electricity, flight or the telephone simply hoarded the gift, and did not share with the world?

In its most practical sense, the word purpose - *the reason for which we exist*, can be viewed as our specific function in the world. If you are good at building things, then perhaps you become a carpenter, engineer or architect. Good with people? Social services may be the path for you. If you are creative then you might find yourself making art, music or films for the enjoyment of others. So whether you are a mortician, psychologist, farmer, builder, medical professional, cook/chef, care taker, electrician, sanitation worker, designer, and on and on, the world needs your specific talents for its survival and existence.

However, on a less practical, and more existential level is where the debate often begins, and where we meet the fork in the road. Are we here solely to fulfill a function or role? What more to life than just existence and survival? Some believe in a higher power, and life after life, while others believe that there is no life after death, and still others believe we have many, many lives to live. I am not here to answer this question, for beliefs run deeply through upbringing, perspective, and even trauma. I would like to invite you, rather, to search your heart to find your purpose here on this planet. This will require times of quiet and deep introspection, study and wisdom seeking.

Whatever you discover, know that, as a human, you will always be on a pursuit to find a purpose to fulfill, whether big or small, practical or existential.

3
MINDFULNESS & HEALING

"You can't stop the waves, but you can learn to surf."

— JON KABAT-ZINN

We now live in a time where terms like wellness, self-awareness, trauma, mental health, and mindfulness are commonplace. It is wonderful to live in a society that no longer steers away from these conversations. When I was growing up, no one was discussing mental health, let alone encouraging each other to go to therapy to "do the work." It is an unfortunate truth that the majority of people have some sort of trauma. Experiences we've had as children or adults that cause us emotional or mental pain. This is nothing to be ashamed of, just a symptom of the human experience. I am a firm believer in therapy and have personally spent many years speaking to a professional about my own childhood traumas. In fact, I even told one of my therapists, she was like a saint, having the desire to listen to other people's problems all day, and that she deserved a medal. What a gift to have people like this in the world. Whatever form of healing you decide to embark upon, whether it is talk therapy, meditation, or just good old-fashioned networks of people who allow you to be yourself without judgment, I strongly believe it is a crucial part of living a full and meaningful life. In this section, we will discuss various paths to healing and mindfulness.

THE TIME BEING

When was the last time you encountered an awe-inspiring, breathtaking moment? Looking into your lover's eyes, an incredible sunset, a full moon, a school of dolphins, an inky sky filled with stars, a snow capped mountain range or sitting next to a crackling fire? It is in these moments that we are reminded of the beauty of life. In these moments, we are at rest.

In our Western culture, we are constantly on the go, focused on making goals, meeting deadlines, and striving for success. We go to work and school, participate in extracurricular activities, attend meetings, dinners, and engagements, we go to shows and parties, engage in projects, make phone calls, and on and on. However, we seldom take time to check in with ourselves, to listen to our soul and spirit, and just ***be***. ***Be***-ing still, ***be***-ing meditative, ***be***-ing alone, ***be***-ing at one with our thoughts. It's even part of our species name, a Human ***Be***-ing. I'll be the first to admit, it is not an easy thing, especially since I am not, by nature, a ***be***-er, but rather a ***do***-er.

Where is the place where you can just ***be***? Is it a bathtub, a mountain top, the ocean side, your bed, a bike, a park bench, a sofa, a swimming pool, a spa, or a massage table? Find a place where you can practice the art and discipline of allowing your mind to be open and free enough to receive thoughts, notions, visions, and inspirations that you would not otherwise be able to hear in the hustle and bustle of your busy life. Wherever it is, find it, and revisit it again and again!

You will be amazed by what you hear when you are quiet and the incredible clarity you will achieve during these times. You want to know where I got the idea for this book, you guessed it, in a time of ***be***-ing (on my bed). You will thank yourself for finding the time and space. No doubt it will help you to ***be***-come a better Human ***Be***ing.

MIND YOUR TIME

As Humans, we have several different states in which our brains operate. There's the alpha, the beta, and the theta.

Alpha is characterized by being clear-headed, present, and fully in the moment. Alpha waves create a sense of peace and well-being in your mind and body. When people are in this state, they seem to exude charisma as their mind focuses only on the here and now.

Beta brain waves are associated with normal waking consciousness and a heightened state of alertness, logic, and critical reasoning. As you go about your daily activities, you are in Beta. It lies at the base of your conscious awareness and is the gateway to your subconscious mind.

Then there is the type of brain activity that we don't talk about much; in fact, it is very easy to dismiss this type of brain activity altogether. The Theta mind is the mysterious border between the conscious and the subconscious worlds. Theta brain waves are the frequencies of the barely conscious state, just before sleeping and just after awakening. It is your mind when it is rested, unpressured, and pliable. The ideation that can occur during the theta state is free-flowing and occurs without censorship or guilt. It is typically a very positive mental state. In the theta state, the mind is capable of deep and profound learning, healing, and growth.

Have you ever awakened at three or four in the morning and couldn't go back to sleep? Lying there, staring at the ceiling, and bada bing bada boom, the best idea you have ever had pops into your brain.

You continue pondering, plotting, planning for a good several minutes, and you think, "Yes, this is the answer to my big problem, the source of all knowledge and understanding." Then you slowly fade back into your sweet slumber, wake up in the morning, and can barely recall those amazing wee morning revelations. It all feels like a distant dream. Wait, was it a dream? No, it wasn't! The problem is you didn't write it down.

Many artists, writers, and musicians experience some of their best moments of creativity, revelations, songs, or book ideas during this state, and many of them keep a notepad or other device nearby so when they awake with these fiery epiphanies, they can write them down. I have many notes on programs I've desired to start, and screenplays I've wanted to write; ideas that came to my theta mind. So the next time you toss and turn and wake up at a strange hour, instead of being frustrated, perhaps take a moment to listen to your mind; it might be trying to tell you something revolutionary.

BACK TO THE FUTURE

The futurist person, in Gallup's *Strengths Finder*, is a personal strength in one of the 34 strength themes. People exceptionally talented in the futuristic theme are motivated by the future and what could be. They are the dreamer, the visionary, and they inspire others with their visions of the future. They have the ability to look beyond what is, to the possibilities of a better product, team, life, and even world.

The benefit of this strength is having the ability to see the big picture. This person is good to have on a team as someone who can forecast trends and has the ability to innovate. This individual is the planner, and someone you want at your picnic because they remembered to bring the trash bags and napkins. They can look at the rundown shack and see their dream home.

As a futuristic person, I am always looking at what can be, but with every strength, there is a flip side. Over the years I have found that I can easily grow discontent in my current situation because I am so preoccupied looking to the future, and planning for what might be, that I have often missed the right now. I tend to be impatient with the natural process through which life unfolds. It has taken many years and great mental discipline to be content with the moment, to see my current blessings, and not long for the what-ifs. The truth of the matter is that the future is promised to no one, and if we are not careful, we will miss the life that is right in front of us because we are so busy trying to live in a time that does not yet exist. My challenge to myself, and to all my fellow futurists is to slow down your mind, pray and hope for the future, but do not forget what is right in front of you.

THE PRECIOUS PRESENT

The wind is gently blowing through your hair. You can taste the salt on your lips. The sound of seagulls off in the distance, and the faint laughter of children rings in your ear. Just as you walk to the water's edge, a family of sandpipers scuffles by and a group of pelicans glides inches above the water. As the sun melts into the horizon, a school of dolphins playfully swims by, chatting and frolicking in the waves.

Now imagine that at this very moment, you were fretting over what you were going to cook for dinner or dwelling on a past conversation. When we are dwelling in the past or longing for the future, we miss what is right in front of us, the present. When handed a gift, who would say at that moment, "I was thinking about what you bought me last year, and it scares me to open this gift because I am afraid I won't like it as much." Or, "Gosh, I am so glad you bought me this, but before I open it, I'd like to say that I am really looking forward to what you buy me next year." How absurd! Life is a gift, and it is each present moment that makes up our memories (the past) and our hopes (the future), but without the present moment, there is no life at all because you are not alive in the past, and you are not alive in the future; you are alive right now. As humans, we are insatiable, always longing for more. You get that position you have been dying for, and as soon as you are in it you are looking for the next best role. We buy homes, cars, vacations, and long for the next home upgrade or new car model. I'm guilty as well. I'll admit that when I'm on vacation, I'm often dreaming about my next adventure. Why is it so important to stay in the present?

The term "mindfulness" has been widely used in this era to define being in the present.

To live mindfully is to be in the moment, rather than dwelling on the past or projecting the future. Part of mindfulness is simply noting what is happening in our immediate surroundings, observing and labeling thoughts, feelings, and sensations in the body in an objective manner, without self-criticism and judgment. Awareness and acceptance are key ingredients within mindfulness. Awareness is the ability to focus on our inner processes and experiences in the moment. Acceptance is the ability to observe and be at peace with — rather than judge or avoid these very streams of thought.

Research also suggests that our experience of time tends to be heavily influenced by our emotional state. Fears and insecurities about the past and the future can make it difficult to fully appreciate the present. The key is learning how to pay attention in the moment.

Some experts suggest you practice mindfulness as you awake, focusing on your breathing and the way your body gradually becomes more energized. You can also incorporate a brief meditation into your workday (perhaps at lunch break) and focus on and appreciate the experience of eating. You can begin by taking deep breaths. Focus on each breath and the sensations of the moment, such as sounds, scents, and the temperature around you. Turn your attention to the thoughts and emotions you are experiencing. Allow each thought to exist without judgment or attaching negativity to it. Sit with those thoughts. The experience may conjure a strong emotional reaction. Exploring that response can be an opportunity to begin to address or resolve underlying issues.

Mindfulness helps us to be grateful for the things we have now, for the people who are in our lives now, for the opportunities we are experiencing now. When we are present, we are less concerned about what was and what will be. We are more joyful and fully showing up in our daily lives. Being present helps us to better enjoy life because we see all the good that is around us, right now. As so wisely and eloquently put by Eleanor Roosevelt, "*Yesterday is history, tomorrow is a mystery, and today is a gift, that is why it is called the present.*"

TIME (*HELPS*) HEAL ALL WOUNDS

Pain is an unfortunate part of the human experience. Not one of us will escape this planet without someone offending us, hurting us, scarring us or inflicting upon us some type of emotional pain. Wounds come from many sources: failed relationships and heartbreak, abuse, loss of loved ones, disappointments, childhood traumas, and people not meeting our expectations. These experiences of past pain shape who we are, but do not define us. Pain properly navigated can serve as a reminder not to repeat the same mistakes.

Some pain is easily resolved with a simple apology, while other pain may take much longer to heal from. It is what we do with our pain that counts. The most important thing about our pasts is that we have passed through, we are on the other side of it, we've survived! We've heard at least one of these clichés, "What doesn't kill you will make you stronger," "When life gives you lemons, make lemonade," "When life closes a door, look for the open window," and on and on.

While I hate to hear these types of pat answers when I am in the midst of my pain, there is a twinge of truth to them. I can't think of a single pain point in my life that hasn't made me wiser, more aware, more patient, gentler, more humble, more compassionate, and more understanding. Would I want to go through the pain again? No way! However, I would not be the person I am today without that pain. I have had my share of lemons, and I can also tell you that my all time favorite beverage is lemonade (true story).

In no way am I saying to ignore your past or to pretend it away, quite the contrary in fact. I am a firm believer in healing and dealing with issues head-on. I also believe that the unresolved pain of our pasts will absolutely haunt us in the present and the future. I have spent many, many hours in therapy dealing with some of the most painful experiences in my life; crying, yelling, and yes, even as a Christian woman, cursing at times. Yet, oh the release and relief of speaking my pain out loud. The healing of the heart and soul that comes after facing the admittedly scary process of tapping into the past and dealing with painful memories is like no other form of relief. What pain have you yet to face? Do you need to forgive someone who has wronged or abused you? Perhaps you need to forgive yourself?

Some people are of the notion that what has passed is the past. They believe they should soldier through the pain, never to talk or think about it again. The problem with this thinking is that even if you are not consciously dealing with those issues, your subconscious is. Wounds pile up, and if not dealt with, they will come out one way or another and play into many facets of your daily life. Have you ever exploded about something that to others may seem very small, and you look up and think, why did that make me so angry? That most likely is anger that is misplaced - an anger about a hurt that you have not yet exposed or dealt with. You keep pushing it down, and pushing it down, hoping it will disappear, but it won't, you won't be healed from it until it is dealt with.

If you slice your finger, it is going to bleed. You may need to go to the doctor and get stitches. If that's the case, you'll come home with a bandage around your finger and instructions on how to manage, clean, and change the bandage. If it is bad enough, the doctor may instruct you not to change the bandage yourself, but to make a follow-up appointment so they can oversee the progress. Once the stitches are removed, you will still need to be careful with the wound. You will need to care for it, monitor it, and protect it. Eventually, the wound will close, and you'll no longer experience tenderness, allowing you to return to your normal life. While there may be a scar, it will eventually heal. The very thing that allowed its complete healing is, you got it, time, and what you did during this time.

A wound that is ignored cannot heal properly. Imagine the person who sliced his finger and needed stitches. Instead of going to the doctor, he just threw a bandage on it, hoping and praying the bleeding would stop. After the bleeding stopped, he did not clean it properly, and it became infected. Let's say he still refused to see a doctor, and now his finger is festering with gangrene. Eventually, the finger would need to be amputated. How ridiculous this sounds, right? Why would someone allow themselves to get to this point, where the amputation of a limb was the ultimate resort?

Now imagine if we ignore the wounds of our hearts and allow metaphorical gangrene to occur. Infections of the heart do not only affect you, but those around you, as they can surface in many unhealthy ways, such as anger and rage, an inability to form close relationships for the sake of "protecting" yourself, a lack of trust, bitterness, anxiety, and depression. If we ignore our pain, it will likely cause us to turn to unhealthy coping mechanisms like overeating, drug and alcohol abuse, or sex addiction.

Since our minds, bodies, and spirits are all connected, undealt with issues can eventually manifest into other such detrimental conditions like heart disease and even cancer. We must care for the wounds of the heart before they become infections of the heart.

4
DREAMING & GOAL SETTING

"So many of our dreams at first seem impossible, then they seem improbable, and then, when we summon the will, they soon become inevitable."

— CHRISTOPHER REEVE

DREAM A LITTLE DREAM

Many Americans are unhappy in the work they do, trapped in jobs for money, titles, and security. While none of these are negative in and of themselves, let's be honest, the vast majority of Americans dread Mondays and live for Fridays. Most of us will spend nearly 30% of our lives laboring. Wouldn't you rather use the five to six days and the forty to fifty hours of your week doing something you love? The saying do what you love and the money will follow, is not necessarily about being wealthy. It's referring to making a living and being fulfilled in the process.

Unfortunately, sometimes what we consider our passion is not what pays the bills, so often it sits on the back shelf. For example, when writing a part of this section, I had already worked almost nine hours at a full-time job, went to the gym, ate dinner, did another quick work task, and then finally had the time to work on my true passion, for a mere 30 minutes at 12:45 a.m. With your passion, you have to find and make the time because it is the thing that energizes you, centers you, gives you peace and joy, which not only benefits you, but also those around you.

It's never too late to discover or pursue your passions and dreams. It wasn't until I was in my 40s that I realized writing was a passion. It wasn't like I hadn't already enjoyed writing. In fact, I had been writing, in some form, my entire adult life. Poetry in my 20s, grant writing in my 30s, and published my first novel in my early 40s. I remember the day like yesterday. I sat at my computer to revise a grant I had written. When I looked up, two hours had passed like it was five minutes. It was at that point I realized that I *loved* writing!

When we ignore our joys and passions, it is similar to when we ignore a food craving. We've all been there. You have a craving for a chocolate bar, but instead, you eat an apple, followed by some peanut butter and almonds, all in the name of being healthy. However, in the end, you still wind up eating that chocolate bar because that's what your body was actually craving. Thus, all along, you consumed unnecessary calories, trying to fight the original craving. Our soul craves what it craves, and it is virtually impossible to find joy when we are constantly suppressing our intended and desired life path. So don't waste your time pursuing the apple and almonds, go for the chocolate bar.

Some people might argue against what I am saying. They may tell you that pursuing a passion is irresponsible or only for the elite. They may advise you to focus on a skill or job that will maximize your earnings or offer the best retirement plan. I think many of us have moved beyond this thinking, having seen the evidence of unfulfilled people who live within this paradigm. If you are swayed by this argument, I challenge you to ask that person how much joy they have in their work. If the answer is none, then you have your answer. Keep the course in finding and pursuing the work that makes you feel alive.

I'll give you an example of a situation where someone took the long route to their dream. My sister is an incredible visual artist. For years, I encouraged her to pursue her art by going to school to continue to hone her skills. Instead, she went to school twice, once for phlebotomy and the second time for medical assisting. She spent loads of money, and after graduating, never stepped foot into a medical facility. Now she does nails and creates incredible paintings. It took her years to pursue it because she tried to go after something that seemed "logical," but it did not make sense to her natural talents, skills, or passions. I'd like to save you the heartache, headache, and dollars, and encourage you to pursue what you love from the start, and the money will follow. It may be a tough road at first, but what in life is easy? A tough road pursuing your dreams versus the tough road of doing work you hate! The choice is yours.

There are entire books on following your dreams, identifying your dreams, and living your dreams. One of my favorite books is called *The Dream Giver*, by Bruce Wilkinson. It is a beautiful parable of a man named Nobody who discovers his dream and then realizes the difficulties he must face in pursuing it.

In his book, Wilkinson discusses how many people don't even know what their dream is, let alone are on a journey to pursue it.

If you are a dreamer, then you may very well have experienced a dream crusher (someone who scoffs at or shoots down your dream). I strongly advise that you only share your dreams with people who you know are going to be supportive, no matter if they agree or understand your dream. A new dream is like a newborn baby. You would not likely hand your newborn child to someone who smells like a chimney after having smoked two cigarettes, and can barely stand on two feet because they've consumed too much alcohol. Same with your dream baby. Hand it only to those whom you have the utmost trust.

FINDING THE DREAM, LIVING THE DREAM OR SOMEWHERE IN BETWEEN

Chances are you are one of four people - someone who has yet to determine their dream, someone who knows and is pursuing their dream, someone who is on the stepping stone, looking across the river at their dream, or someone who is living their dream.

Are you someone who is still trying to ***find your dream?*** Until you discover what makes you, you, your life may feel dull or unfulfilled. This self-discovery process is not an overnight one, but trust me, the exploration is worth it when you finally hit the proverbial nail on the head in identifying your dream.

A big part of this self-discovery journey is identifying what it is that truly brings you joy. What are some activities you love to immerse yourself in? Maybe you restore old cars, perhaps it's crafting, baking, cooking, sewing, painting, photography, music, designing, athletics, science, or running a business. Are you a builder of things, a healer, scientist, speaker, teacher, writer, performer, musician? Maybe you're a theorist, philosopher, or mental health professional. Whatever it is that you have been gifted with, whatever your "specialty," time is a factor in how you pursue that which is most unique to you.

During the process of self-discovery, it is essential to pay attention to that little voice within. It is not a loud voice; it is a small whisper that can easily be beaten back and ignored by the demands of life and the opinions of friends, family, and society. Part of the process includes paying attention to the clues that your life has already given you. As a child, what did you spend much of your time doing? What activities make your heart smile and light you up? What is something you would do even if it didn't pay? These are all clues about things you love. The problem is when we ignore these clues.

So you have figured out what it is, and now you are on the road to actively ***pursuing your dream***. Perhaps you have decided to go back to school so that you can pursue that new career, or maybe you have decided to leave behind a full time job to start a business. If this is you, you know that it has not been an easy journey thus far. In his book, *The Dream Giver,* Bruce Wilkinson talks about being in a valley as a normal and expected time on your pursuit. What is generally happening in the valley is that lessons are being learned that will produce insight, perseverance, wisdom, and the tools necessary to succeed at your dream. Valleys can look like not having the necessary resources, closed doors and rejection, or the loss of the initial energy or motivation. This is the place where most people give up on the dream, but if you persevere, friend, you will find yourself on the other side of that valley and approaching the mountain top. Remember, however, that it is impossible to get to the top of a mountain without pain, endurance, and intense effort, but once you do, oh the view!

Name one successful person (famous or not) who said their dream just fell into their lap, without struggle. Oprah Winfrey was once told she didn't have a face for TV, yet she is now one of just a handful of billionaire women in the world. Walt Disney went bankrupt on numerous occasions, and was told no 300 times by a number of banks before successfully launching what we know now to be a multi-billion dollar enterprise.

What about those who have made a difference fighting the thankless battle for the disenfranchised, like Harriet Tubman, The Suffragettes, Martin Luther King, Mother Teresa, Gandhi, Jesus? These people fought for human rights and were up against major opposition, even to the point of losing their lives for what they believed. How about the countless men and women who have started and lost businesses, athletes who push themselves to make it to the top of their game, and people who decided to leave their country of origin on a quest for a better life? These, and countless other artists, inventors, creators, scientists, and the like, who pushed through the setbacks, have produced some of the most wonderful things that you and I get to experience today.

Ask yourself what is stopping you from pressing on toward your goal and your dream. What obstacle is in your way, and how will you decide to move past it toward perseverance? If it is really your dream, don't give up! Keep dreaming, keep striving.

You have accomplished a great deal if you have made it this far in the pursuit of your dream. You have identified it, and set out to make the right moves to set it in motion. However, you still feel far from living it out, and are on what seems to be a continual path of self-development. I'd like to call you someone who is on the ***stepping stone to your dream***. You have successfully done many of the necessary, and seemingly peripheral efforts. Maybe you have gone back to school, taken a training course, and self-taught through "YouTube University." Perhaps you have even taken a stab at the actual dream itself, but it feels like you are on a continual treadmill of training. Trust me when I say I have been here, and in many ways, I am still here. I have said on many occasions I feel like I am on the bench, begging for the coach to put me in the game. We'll talk about this in a little more depth in the next section, in addition to the section of this book entitled *Time you Can't Control*, but suffice it to say that it takes time to fully actualize a dream. Primarily because we need preparation, and that preparation is not solely related to skills or abilities, but also to maturity to be able to handle your dream on a mental and emotional level.

If you are the person ***living your dream***, I want to say a huge CONGRATULATION to you!! You could probably write a book of your own from all the lessons learned on your journey. You know what it means to fight through fear, overcome the time in the valley, and push past the naysayers. You have persisted, cried, and even wanted to give up at times, but you didn't. Keep up the great work!

"INSTA"- GRATIFICATION

We are living in an age where things can be accomplished in nanoseconds. We can order our food, our transportation, and household items with a swipe of a finger. We can change the way we look with a filter, and now with AI, things are moving into a whole new realm. It is no wonder we also expect instant success. However, no matter how fast a computer can move, it does not change the fact that there is a process for achievement. Life is not the Internet; it's not high speed. Life unfolds and everything we do takes time to process. If you plant a seed in the ground, you're not going to have a tree in a week. It takes time for it to grow and mature before you will ever see fruit. The same is true with anything in life, including your dreams and goals. You can try to rush them, but you will inevitably be frustrated at every turn.

I have heard the quote on many different platforms: "It took me 10 years to become an overnight success." Talk to any actor, writer, singer, athlete, entrepreneur, and they will fill in the blanks for you of the years they struggled, trained, and received rejections. For some, accomplishing a goal can take months, years, decades or even a lifetime. Sure, it may seem like they made it overnight because by the time we see them, they have "arrived." There is nothing great that we can achieve without sweat, tears, overcoming fears, and toil. In this process of preparation, we are building the necessary character and skills to make our dreams a reality.

Some of us have known the path we are supposed to take from a very early age. We have looked from a hilltop across the promised land at a dream that was off into the distance. Before we can reach it, we have to travel to it. Along the way, we will encounter valleys, peaks, rivers, marshes, desert lands, and labyrinths, not to mention all the perilous people we need to avoid.

The story of Joseph, in the Old Testament, has always resonated with me, on this front. Joseph was a dreamer. When he was merely 17 years old, he dreamt that the sun, the moon, and twelve stars were bowing down to him. This signified his mother, father, and all of his brothers. For sharing his dream, his father rebuked him. His brothers, already jealous of him, thought to kill him, but instead decided to sell him into slavery. Talk about family dysfunction! In the household where he was serving, his master had the utmost confidence in Joseph and put him in charge of all things. Being that he was very handsome, the wife of the master took notice of him. She attempted, on several occasions, to seduce him, but he refused to do such a thing with his boss' wife. She became angry at his rebuff and falsely accused him of taking advantage of her. For this, Joseph was imprisoned.

While in prison, Joseph gained favor with the warden. One day, he interpreted a dream for a fellow inmate, Pharaoh's baker. The dream signified that the baker would soon be released from prison. For this, Joseph asked in return that the baker would remember him once he was freed, but he forgot Joseph, which cost him another two years in prison. It was in this place of "hiding" that served as Joseph's training grounds. The place where no one knew him or his name, let alone his significance, was the place that would train him for his future role and responsibilities.

Fast forward to the time Joseph actually saw the realization of his original dream, he was now in his 30s. He was instated as the second in command to Pharaoh, after interpreting his dream about an impending famine. At 17 years old, Joseph was given his destiny, but it took decades for that dream to become a reality. As a teenager, he did not have the wisdom nor the life experience to handle such a role, and likely would have failed. The same is true for us; without the time and the years of preparation, we would be underdeveloped and ill-prepared for the big dream that lies within our hearts.

At the age of 14, I knew I'd be an entrepreneur, and at 18, I understood that one day I'd be a philanthropist. Since discovering these dreams I have done everything in my power to draw closer to that reality, including, on the business side, joining the Future Business Leaders of America club in high school (I'm most certainly a nerd), majoring in business in my first two years of college, reading marketing textbooks, for fun, and attending marketing and leadership classes and seminars. I left a full-time job in 2008 to start a business. However, I had to take a full-time job in 2011 to make ends meet. Then, in 2016, I left that job to start yet another business, all in pursuit of entrepreneurialism. Even though neither of those businesses exists today, I can tell you that I learned so much during those experiences!

In an effort to pursue my dream of philanthropy, I have made numerous strides in that vein, from getting my Master's in administrative Social Work to working in a variety of roles at a number of nonprofits, serving under-resourced groups and individuals. I give to a variety of charities, and have written proposals for programs I hope to start one day.

Imagine if at 14 I was a business owner and at 18 a philanthropist. I would have been able to say that I achieved my dream. Yet, at those ages, I would have lacked the emotional, mental, and experiential maturity to carry out those roles sufficiently. It was only then that the seeds of those dreams were planted, but I have needed years, rather decades, to be in a place where I can fully handle what it is that I am being called to do and to be.

The time that may feel like a waste is actually the time that is most valuable and necessary to prepare you to step into your greatness. It is the time essential for you to become who you were meant to be. Preparing you to handle the task for which you were called. The skills you are learning, the connections you are making, and the experiences you are having are all necessary for the future of your dream. The process may feel long and never-ending, but like Joseph, the struggles we endure along the way are essential elements that prepare us to step into our destiny.

THE DARK SIDE OF THE MOON

I've heard it so many times before, "Shoot for the moon, and you will land among the stars." What if you don't have enough energy, on your dream journey, to shoot for the street light?

For those of us who consider ourselves to be dreamers, it can feel like a long, daunting, and often lonely road. There are times when I genuinely wish I weren't a dreamer, and that I could be satisfied with working for someone else, taking my two-week annual vacation, and living for the weekends.

I have wanted to throw in the towel of discouragement more times than I can count. I have had countless conversations with myself and loved ones about feeling ridiculous for giving up a reliable job, career path, and financial stability to pursue my passions. There are times I have felt foolish and misunderstood. I have hit more roadblocks, been told no more times than I can count, sacrificed my time, energy, money, and sometimes what feels like my sanity to pursue the dream. On numerous occasions, I have even forgone my own desires by opting out of events, trips, and experiences due to lack of finances, all in the name of my pursuit. Can you relate?

During these dispirited times, the question, "*Why?*" has often come up. Why am I doing this? Why don't I just get a regular nine-to-five job? Why do I keep torturing myself? When I can sit in the calm and remind myself of the answer to my *why,* it puts wind back in my sails. I remind myself that my objective is to eventually use my wealth (that I don't yet possess) to create a foundation, programs, and opportunities that will benefit some of the country's most marginalized and vulnerable individuals, a dream that was put on my heart when I was 18 years old. What is your *why*? Do you know? If not, then it will likely be very easy to give up when times get hard, and believe me, they will.

Your *why* is the location on the map with the big X on it. So when your compass needle starts to spin out of control, you will need to get it back to North. Without knowing *why,* throwing in the proverbial towel is much more of an option. When you know your *why*, you may get knocked down, dismayed, and feel like quitting, but you have a clear direction that will set you back on course.

In addition to knowing your big *why,* it is essential to find solace during those low points in your dream journey. Some ways of doing this would be to find like-minded individuals or groups that either have a direct correlation to your dream, or simply other dreamers to connect with. I have found that surrounding myself with other creatives, writers, artists, and entrepreneurs helps to normalize my situation. Not only this, but when you surround yourself with others, you naturally become more buoyant, gleaning inspiration, encouragement, tips, support, and even opportunities.

Over the years, it has helped me to write at cafes because it is there that other writers and entrepreneurs often dwell, and while we may not utter a single word to one another, I know I am surrounded by similar people.

Other ways to help uplift your dreamer soul is to feed it. This can happen through listening to podcasts (either around your area of emphasis or simply other people pursuing a passion), reading articles, listening to webinars, or attending conferences.

At the end of the day, as a dreamer, you will get discouraged and knocked down. When that happens —or even better, before it does —it is crucial to pour into yourself to fortify your efforts, mind, and soul.

THE DREAM CATCHER

I have designed a tool called ***The Dream Catcher*** (See diagram below & Appendix for blank version), borrowing from the Native American craft created during the 1960s Pan-Indian movement. The purpose of the dream catcher was to catch evil spirits and bad dreams during the night, and thus it was commonly hung above the bed.

The tool I have created takes this Native creation and couples it with the widely-known Japanese concept of Ikigai (ee-key-guy). *Iki,* which means "life" and *gai* meaning "worth." When combined, the words mean that which gives your life worth, meaning or purpose. In essence, Ikigai refers to defining your personal life meaning as it relates to your talents, passions, and profession, in addition to what you can give to the wider world.

The Dream Catcher tool will help to synthesize your *passions, natural-born talents,* and *skills* all in one place so that you can find some intersectionalities and commonalities between these three areas, utilizing a common device called the Venn Diagram, created in 1880 by John Venn.

Passions include that which brings you joy and makes your heart sing. Passions are often activities that we lose ourselves in, with respect to time. You may have a passion for singing, teaching, the ocean, traveling, cooking, and on and on. Most people have a number of passions.

Natural Born Talents (also known as strengths or gifts), are areas in which you excel with minimal thought or effort. It's that one thing that other people may consistently seek your expertise or assistance for.

Skills & Abilities are areas that we generally have cultivated through education and training, whether formally, on the job, or simply in our lived experiences. In these areas, you may have certifications, degrees, or work experience. These areas often show up on your resume.

You may be 'passionate & talented', 'talented & skilled', 'passionate & skilled' or 'passionate, talented, & skilled' in several areas. These are the areas you will want to further explore as you continue on your path to discovering your dreams.

First, take a moment to use the *Passions, Talents & Skills* Worksheet (See Appendix) to tease out your lists before adding the entries directly to ***The Dream Catcher*** (See graph below).

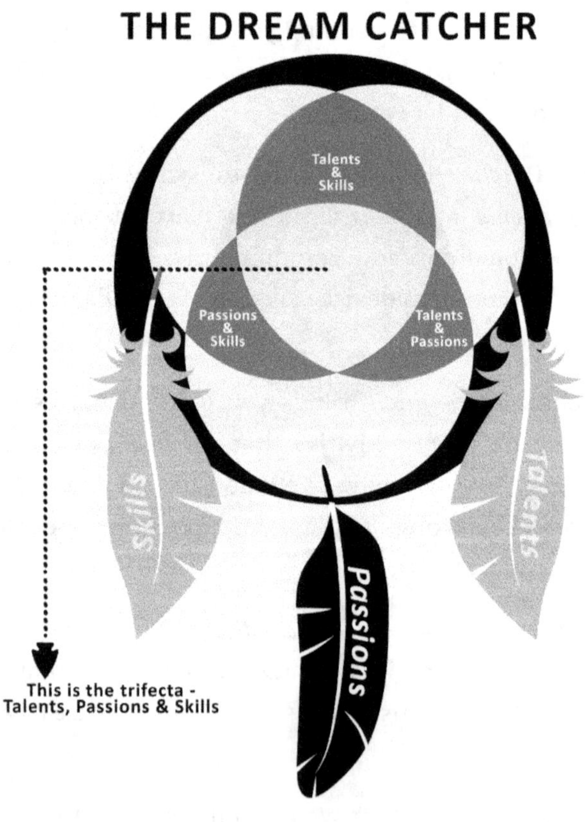

THE DREAM CATCHER

Talents & Skills

Passions & Skills

Talents & Passions

Skills

Talents

Passions

This is the trifecta - Talents, Passions & Skills

STOP & SMELL THE ROSES

Much like how we cannot achieve success overnight, we must also realize that at the end of the day, the attainment of that success can often be a fleeting moment in time. We mustn't forget about the journey that it takes to get there, or you might miss some beautiful moments along the way. There was a scene in the movie *Soul*, where the lead character was finally asked to perform at the jazz club with one of his musical idols. After the day was over, he asked, "So what next?" His idol said, "You come back tomorrow, and the day after that." He was crestfallen because the attainment of his goal almost felt like a letdown in comparison to the desire of it, which he had chased for so long.

If you are a goal-oriented person, like myself, I am talking to you. While it is imperative to keep the goal in mind as you work through all the necessary steps to get there, if you rush past the interim, you are likely going to find the process quite miserable. I have heard the quote over and over, "It's not the outcome, but the journey that counts," or "It's about the process, not the prize." To be completely real, these statements used to make me cringe. I rolled my eyes and would think, whoever came up with that quote must not ever finish anything. It has only been in the last few years that I have started to embrace this notion of relishing the journey.

When we are in a constant state of asking "What's next?", we enter a game of chasing that next shiny object, which can lead to an insatiable desire for more check marks and finished assignments, and in the process, we miss some wonderful moments of personal growth on the road to hitting that mark.

Think for a moment about a marathon runner. For weeks, months, and even up to a year before the actual race, they are in training, running upwards of 10, 15, and even 20 miles a day. They may even have run a marathon before the day of the official race. Their training *journey* is the very thing that got them to that day in the first place.

Without it, there is no way they would be able to successfully finish the race. Of course, it is important to finish what we start, but when we are hung up on the outcome, we genuinely miss out on the benefits of the lessons learned, the discipline gained, and the nuggets of wisdom brought forth by the training.

In an interview with the famous filmmaker, Martin Scorsese, he once said, *"I miss the time when I had the desire to experiment, and try different kinds of films, I miss that time, but that's done, it's over. There is an obligation as you get older, you have a family."*

Have you ever actually stopped and smelled a rose? The first time I did it I understood completely why that person made up that saying. I received an incredible endorphin rush, a truly natural high, not to mention the wonderful fragrance. This is one of the reasons I love walking so much. In the car, on the way to our destination, we speed past everything, set on a mission to reach our destination. On a walk, however, you see everything. Children playing, beautifully blooming flowers, trees, birds, bees, kitties, doggies, beautifully landscaped homes, and on and on. If we approach life more like the walker than the driver, we will experience so many more wonderful little things that life has to offer.

Whether you are trying to run a race, complete a book, graduate from college, paint a masterpiece, or get a promotion, take the time to see the joy that not only comes from attaining the goal, but also to celebrate the hard work and the process that led you up to the point.

5
PERSONAL GROWTH & DEVELOPMENT

"Do the best you can until you know better. Then when you know better, do better."

— MAYA ANGELOU

A TIME TO GROW

Anything good takes time to mature: trees, fine wine, cheese. Humans are in no way exempt from the time necessary to mature and gain wisdom. We do know, however, that age does not automatically equal maturity. I have known many people who are in the later stages of life, and still have not grown in certain areas. Quite frankly, they are stuck. Whether stuck in their flaws or in their pride.

Maturing takes humility and the willingness to learn from our mistakes. It takes getting and pursuing feedback from others so that we can uncover our blind spots. Trust me when I say that if we don't get the lesson the first or second time, it will continue to roll around, until we do, however long that may take. Heaven forbid we deal with the same lesson our whole life, ignoring the signals, and refusing the invitation to change.

I mention one of my aunts a lot because she is one person who has been a great guide for life lessons. On a number of occasions, she told me that life is like a spiral staircase; we keep coming back around to many of the same themes. However, as time passes and the higher we are on the staircase, it is our vantage point and perspective that change.

Maturing does not happen in a vacuum. We can ask for wisdom, but it will never just fall out of the sky, and ta-da, we are magically transformed. Growth and maturity come through struggle, situations, and circumstances that we must face in order to push past our natural tendencies, challenging us to become different, and hence, more mature.

TUMMY TIME

Despite the fact that I don't have children of my own, I am familiar with the concept of tummy time. It's a period that you place your infant on their belly, while awake, and supervised. This allows them to change to a different position other than on their back, which over time can produce flat spots on their heads. Tummy time also helps a baby develop strong neck and shoulder muscles, and promotes motor skills, all of which are necessary for activities like sitting up, rolling over, crawling, and walking.

If you're reading this, of course, you are long past those days. However, as adults, we can participate in a different version of tummy time, which for us is a time for growth and personal development in an effort to strengthen and reinforce our careers or crafts. Examples of this could be participating in seminars and webinars, attending a conference or workshop, taking an online course, listening to podcasts or Ted Talks, or reading articles. Take your tummy time seriously; it's a sure way to foster growth.

MARKING MILESTONES & CELEBRATING VICTORIES

One of the things that has stood out to me over time in my study of the Bible is when, in the Old Testament, people would build physical tributes to commemorate victories they witnessed or specific prayers that were answered. We see this in modern times with the building of statues, monuments, and other memorials. In everyday life, we use trophies, plaques, and certifications.

If we don't take the time to mark our victories, they can easily become forgotten moments of the past. Most of us celebrate momentous occasions like weddings, graduations, births and birthdays, but what about the smaller things like the answered prayer, the new job, the finished project, conquering a physical feat, pounds shed, the ceasing of an unhealthy habit? While we may not likely build a physical monument or receive a trophy for these types of accomplishments, there are ways in which we can commemorate these achievements. Perhaps you are trying to shed a few pounds. A great way to celebrate is to buy yourself a new article of clothing for every five pounds you lose. Maybe you pushed yourself to run that extra mile, despite being tired. Why not reward yourself with a professional foot massage?

In addition to celebrating the actual goal, we should also honor the small wins along the way to the goal. We often become so fixated with the finish line that we diminish progress. Being halfway to a goal is being 50% there, a far cry from 0%, and that is worthy of recognition. If you're training for a marathon, and you hit the 13-mile mark, commend that. You're looking to lose 50 pounds and you've lost 25 so far, revel in it!

I was recently spending time with my cousin. She told me that she was working on her eating, and I told her it showed, and that she looked like she was getting really close to her high school weight (maybe 10-12 pounds, and she would have been there). There was another person with us who quickly disputed my commendation by saying, "No, she's not." I rebuffed her by saying, "Yes, she is close. I did not say she was ***at*** her high school weight, I said she was close, and that is worth recognizing."

Why are we so hard on ourselves? Why have we been trained, as a society, to only celebrate the big triumphs? It doesn't have to be all or nothing.

After each day, each week, each month, and each year, I look back and applaud myself for the work I have done, and all my accomplishments. If we don't, then we are at risk of living a life that is never fully satisfied, constantly striving, and grinding, always looking for the next shiny thing, but never actually arriving.

I have recently started to keep an answered prayers journal, so that I can go back at the end of the year and see all that has come to fruition. If prayer isn't your thing, consider keeping a journal to record all the beautiful, wonderful experiences you've had in a day, week, month, or year. There are many ways to pay tribute to the victories in our lives. Choose what works best for you. The most important thing is that you remember to not forget.

6

TIME FOR RELATIONSHIPS

"The best time to make friends is before you need them."

— ETHEL BARRYMORE

No person is an island. We need each other. Who do you call when you have good news or need a shoulder to cry on? Even for the most fiercely independent or busy individual, relationships are crucial for being a successful human.

SHARING TIME

My friends and family play an essential role in my life, and without them, I would certainly not be the person I am today. In the book *The Five Love Languages,* author Gary Chapman discusses ways in which humans feel loved. Quality time, being one of them, is at the top of my list. This is something that significant people in my life can do to help me feel their love. To be clear, it is not "quantity" time, it is *quality* time. Even if I have a one-hour conversation with someone on the phone, I am bound to feel closer to them.

In the past I have had people feel hurt about the fact that I would pencil them into my calendar. However, my goal in doing this was always so that I could ensure I had the proper, undivided time for them. It is not to say I never have impromptu times with the people in my life, but for someone who often has a lot going on, it has proven to be the best way to provide the wholehearted time the people in my life deserve. In the midst of these times, we connect, catch up, get and give advice, share victories and defeats, and encourage one another.

On the other end of this spectrum, we have heard from numerous entertainer couples that the reason the relationship did not work is because they were away from each other so much (e.g. music tours, filming), and thus the demise of the relationship. If quality time is a necessary part of your relationship's health, be sure to carve it out.

When I was younger, I did not fully have a grasp on love languages. I had a really hard time with simply "hanging out," and when someone asked, I'd often feel like I was wasting precious time that I could be using to "accomplish" something. As a natural "doer" I still find myself wanting to spend time *doing* something, and not simply sitting on the sofa talking, but I equally realize there is a time and a place for that too. By and large, I would say that I like my hang times to be somewhat productive, if possible. For instance, if I have to go to the mall, I may invite a friend who I know likes shopping, or if I plan to take a walk, I'll invite a friend who likes to be active. I even have a friend with whom I watch some of my favorite shows. Incorporating my relationships into my daily activities helps me to feel like I am accomplishing two things: building bonds through quality time, while simultaneously accomplishing something.

If you're like me and need to feel a sense of accomplishment while spending time with loved ones, here is a list of some potential activities:

1. Grocery shopping
2. Trip to the laundromat
3. Exercising - at the gym, walking, hiking, doing yoga, swimming, bike riding
4. Working at a coffee shop
5. Watching your favorite TV show(s)/films
6. Getting a bite to eat (because we all have to eat, right?)
7. Going to a church or religious service/praying together
8. Working on a joint venture/project
9. Joining boards of directors with like-minded friends or family
10. Starting a business
11. Celebrating birthdays
12. Investing together (real estate, business ventures, etc.)
13. Making your annual vision board
14. Meal prepping
15. Getting mani/pedis
16. Helping someone pack their home for a move
17. Studying
18. Taking a class

KNOW WHEN TO FOLD EM'

In the name of not quitting, sometimes we hold on to things for much longer than we should. This can be in the realm of a job, romantic relationship, living situation, business endeavor, and so on. I have seen people stay in relationships for fear of not hurting someone's feelings, not wanting to rock the boat, or the dread of not finding something better.

We need to ask the hard questions. Are these people a help or a hindrance to me? Do they tend to engage in negative, venomous talk, or are they a know-it-all? Are they demanding, demeaning, or otherwise causing you anxiety? Or are they filled with love, light, warmth, and positive inspiration? Ask yourself, do they help me to be a better version of myself, or do they bring out the worst in me? Do they encourage me to pursue my goals or dissuade me from following my passions?

Once you have assessed this, then you have decisions to make. In her book, *Good Boundaries and Goodbyes*, Lysa TerKeurst goes into great depth about the topic of creating boundaries with the people you love. Of course, you most likely will not completely "unfriend" your family. However, you can certainly decide to spend less time with them if that is the healthiest choice. You don't need to completely drop your friends either, unless of course you feel it wise. The idea here is that you create better boundaries around what is and isn't acceptable for you. If this person depletes rather than feeds your soul, then perhaps you begin to create some distance. For example, if you have a friend with whom you need to create some space, instead of spending half the day together, leaving you drained, maybe you decide, before your next conversation, that you will only talk to them for a set amount of time, at which point you then politely excuse yourself from conversation once it starts to take a turn. If necessary, you might feel the need to eventually wean yourself from them altogether, if that is what the situation calls for. Sometimes people simply fall off on their own, and other times we need to make the decision to distance ourselves. If you feel like the friendship is worth salvaging, then you will likely need to have a heart-to-heart conversation about the way you feel in their presence. The people whose lives you are in are probably asking the same questions about you, as they should. What kind of friend are you?

Our time on Earth is short. Too short to allow it to be filled with negative things. It's up to you how you fill your calendar, and who you decide to either collect or discard from your life. It goes well beyond "not hurting someone's feelings," but is much more about doing what is best for your heart, your soul, and your life.

A TIME FOR WAR AND A TIME FOR PEACE

Ecclesiastes so wisely says that there is a time for peace and a time for war. Have you ever known someone who is "always right?" A person is bound to have the last word in any argument. They may even go to the lengths to research a point just so they can "circle back" to let you know they, indeed, were right.

Do you enjoy spending time with this person? The likely answer is no. Regardless of whether or not they are right, this type of behavior is not conducive to healthy, vibrant relationships. It only pushes people away.

If this person is you, you may need to do some introspection and ask yourself, "Why do I feel the need to always be right?" Is it because of some deep insecurity that developed from the past? Maybe a teacher, parent, or peer once told you that you were not smart, and now, subconsciously, there is a deep need to prove that you are. Whatever the root cause, when it comes to mending relationships, aiming for its unification is far more rewarding than being right.

Envision an argument that has erupted amongst a couple. They go back and forth about the facts, and neither is willing to take the first step toward conceding; there will be a stalemate. Now one person is sleeping on the sofa and engaged in the silent treatment. This goes on for days. The Cold War will not cease until someone is willing to end it and make peace. This requires great humility. The person who takes the first step in making the truce may very well be the person who was "right." However, because they value the relationship, they will choose reconciliation over being right, in an effort to restore the peace in their home. Generally, humility begets humility, and once one person takes this step, it disarms the other person.

Try it on for size. Be the first person to admit wrong and to apologize to a loved one.

SEEK UNDERSTANDING

Stephen Covey has coined a very famous quote, "We judge others by their actions, but we want to be judged by our intentions." Ever find yourself in an argument where you cannot seem to get the other person to understand your intentions, or vice versa? This is because, often, when we argue, our goal is generally to get our point across and be understood, rather than to understand the other person, especially if hurt feelings are involved. This is yet another reference to Covey's principle number five, "Seek First to Understand, then to be Understood." Essentially, when we choose to find the cause of someone's behavior we not only have a better understanding, but quite often more compassion and empathy. Even if you still disagree, at the very least, you will have a deeper appreciation of their thought process, and the why behind what they do, and how they think.

Let's take the COVID-19 pandemic of 2020. There were many schools of thought and a varying degree of concern over the issue. There was anything from people who did not dare step outside of their homes to those who refused to wear a face covering, and everything in between.

A family member of mine chose not to spend Thanksgiving with us because she didn't want to wear a mask in the house. She was of the mind that we will all get this disease at some point, and we may as well just accept that and live our normal lives. However, my mother, being older, wanted to take precautions for her health. When Christmas rolled around, I was willing to concede to having her over, not requiring her to wear a mask, although my mother would. We kept the windows open for circulation and instituted social distancing during dinner. Before she arrived I mentioned that we asked, at the very least, to wear a mask in the bathroom and the kitchen areas.

Upon her arrival, I reminded her of this request, but she was clearly offended and annoyed by it. At one point, she contemplated leaving altogether. I was very upset about this and told my mother to just let her go. I felt disrespected in my home, and believed the request was more than a fair compromise. We literally had to have a sit-down to be able to settle the dispute. I was coming from one place and she was coming from another. Before the sit-down, it occurred to me that I should ask how she viewed the pandemic. We opened the conversation with everyone going around and sharing their views. The exercise was quite helpful for de-escalating a potentially disastrous situation. She felt heard, and I felt heard. In the end, our requests were honored, and we had a lovely celebration.

The few moments it took to seek first to understand did not take much time or effort, but the results were resoundingly successful.

Take the time to understand the people around you, what makes them tick? Why do they do what they do? You will be surprised at what you learn, and how many arguments you can avoid.

TIME FOR KINDNESS

There are over 10 million people in the Los Angeles area, and it seems like there are 20 million cars on the road. Driving here is truly the wild, wild west. Some people spend hours commuting to and from work. People are on edge and can be very selfish on the road. Road rage is real. When I moved from Los Angeles to Denver, Colorado, I remember the first time someone allowed me to merge in front of them. It took a moment to realize what was going on, and when I noticed they had intentionally slowed down so that I could make my lane change, I was floored. I vigorously waved thank you, and thought, "I'm not in LA anymore, Toto."

How long did it take that person to pause and offer that act of kindness? Seconds, really, but it left a lasting impression on me. Whether you believe in karma or in the golden rule - "Do unto others as you'd have them do unto you" - or simply have an attitude of quid pro quo, when we do good, good comes back to us, it all relates to treating people with kindness and respect.

It is these kindnesses that make for a happier, healthier mindset, community, and society. I can think of a few other instances where acts of kindness, or lack thereof, have left lasting impressions.

My mother and I ran a small business selling a product she invented. At times, we sold at various events and expos. The day before a particular expo, we arrived to set up our booth. Just two stalls down, a celebrity and her husband were also setting up. The expo lasted two days. All the neighboring vendors were very friendly, making small talk and learning about one another's businesses. In contrast, the celebrity, for the entire time, did not utter a word to us. She barely even looked in our direction. I had seen one of the films she starred in, and up until that point, I thought fairly highly of her. However, after being completely ignored for three days, it was evident to me that she did not feel we were worth her time. It literally would have taken seconds for her to say hello, even if only for the purpose of creating new customers for her product, which was something I would have absolutely used and spread the word about. Instead, the encounter left me with a bad taste in my mouth, and I couldn't even tell you the name of the product.

Another, much more sad example of lacking kindness is a well-known case that occurred in 1964. A woman by the name of Kitty Genovese was brutally murdered outside of her New York apartment. The case was so impactful that her name is often associated with what psychologists have termed Bystander Syndrome - which often happens when we diffuse responsibility (especially in larger cities) by thinking, "Someone else will...call, say something, do something, help." Kitty had arrived home in the early morning hours when she was accosted by a man with a knife who proceeded to stab her. She screamed, and a neighbor's apartment light flicked on, so the assailant fled, but when he saw no one came to her aid, he continued his attack. Thirty-seven people in total witnessed her murder, and not one did anything to help. It would have been far better for the police to have received 37 calls regarding an attempted murder than no calls for a completed one.

Let's end on a high note. One Sunday morning, when I was living in Denver, CO, I was on my way to church. I had to arrive a little early because I was singing that day, and I was running a little late. As I sat at a red light, I noticed, in my rearview mirror, an older man crawling on all fours in a dirt patch just off the sidewalk near the freeway entrance. I reasoned he must have fallen and was struggling to get back up. I saw cars passing in his direction, but probably too fast to notice. I knew turning back would make me late for song practice, but I couldn't bear the thought of being the only one who saw what was happening and didn't do anything about it. Once my light turned green, I made a U-turn. By the time I reached him, I could tell he was disoriented and probably a little embarrassed. Moments later, another car pulled up behind mine.

With these other good Samaritans, we helped the man to his feet. My stopping only cost me about five to 10 minutes, and while I was a few minutes late to song practice, everyone was completely understanding. I am not telling this story to toot my own horn. I tell the story to say, it doesn't take much to show an act of kindness, maybe a few minutes of your time, but in doing so, you could make someone's day or even save a life.

Principle #1 Summary

- We get to choose how we interact with time. Whether you are a morning lark or a night owl, a planner or a by-the-seat-of-your-pantser, time is experienced on an individual level. Knowing how you view time is a crucial first step into the future of how you choose to relate to it.

- Many of us have regrets and desires to re-do the past, while recreating the past is not possible, we can certainly move forward into the future, living a regret-free life.
- Each of us has experienced pain, loss, or trauma of some kind in this life. Taking the time to find ways to heal is essential for living a healthy and fulfilling life.
- Time stands still for no one. If you have a dream you have been wanting to pursue, why wait? Take charge of your life and go after your goals, and that which brings you joy.
- In our human experience, we are all on a journey of self-discovery, learning, and growth. Let's show up with compassion for others as we share this common existence.

Putting Principle #1 Into Practice

1. When are you at your most optimal (when is your prime time)?
2. What time of year do you feel most alive and invigorated?
3. If you could do anything at all, without fear of judgment or criticism, what would it be?
4. How would you feel about your life if you could do this one thing (your answer to #3)?
5. What, if any, are your biggest life regrets? With this knowledge of past regrets, what are some things you are unwilling to allow to become regrets as you move forward?
6. On a scale of 1-10 (1 being the lowest and 10 being the highest), how would you rate your ability to just "***be***?" If you scored 6 or lower, what are some things you can implement into your day, week, or month to focus more on simply ***be***-ing?

7. What are some unhealed areas in your life? How do you plan to seek that healing? Who do you plan to include in the healing process?
8. Have you identified your big dream? If not, take some time to utilize the *Passions, Talents & Skills Worksheet*, and ***The Dream Catcher*** to flesh this out (See Appendix).
9. If you have identified your dream, where are you in the pursuit process (i.e. well on your way, in a valley)? If you are feeling discouraged in the pursuit process, what do you plan to do so that discouragement does not become your stopping point?
10. Who are your dearest relationships? Do you feel you take enough time to nurture those relationships? If not, how can you implement moments of time to strengthen and fortify those relationships?

Challenge: Identify one area of this principle where you feel you can use the most growth. Take some time to reflect and create a plan for forward momentum.

PRINCIPLE #2 : KNOWING THE DIFFERENCE BETWEEN THE TIME YOU CAN CONTROL & THE TIME YOU CANNOT

> *"When we are no longer able to change a situation, we are challenged to change ourselves."*
>
> — VIKTOR FRANKL

We can control our conscious thoughts, how we react, and how we view life. We can control our actions, and whether or not we respond from a place of fear, scarcity, anger or from a place of gratitude, peace, love, and joy. We can project numbers, make plans, set forth goals, and strive. However, there are quite possibly just as many, if not more, factors in life that we cannot control. For example, our DNA, natural-born abilities and intellect, our birthplace, to whom we are born, the siblings and family we were born into, or our language of origin. In fact, we don't know what's going to happen the minute we step outside of our home each day.

I cannot count how many stories I've heard about someone's sports career ending because of an untimely injury. Sometimes it is a relationship that takes an unexpected turn. Perhaps it's a health issue that affects us or our loved ones. Much of the time issues such as these completely shift our life plans. What do we do then?

How is it that our meticulously planned life can so easily be turned upside down? It's so easy to think things like, "This is not fair" or "Why is this happening to me?" We may not ever get the answer we want. I have learned the value of asking "what" instead of why. What am I supposed to learn from this situation? What is my takeaway? What in my character is lacking that this situation will provide?

While we can control the input - what we do, create, and sow into our lives, we cannot, however, control the outcome. If we are not careful to surrender when these uncontrolled instances occur, we can easily become frustrated, angry, and even bitter. How do you respond when things don't go according to plan?

In this section, we will examine ways to find peace by relinquishing our need for control and making space for personal growth.

7
DEALING WITH LIFE PAUSES & ADVERSITY

"Rock bottom became the solid foundation on which I rebuilt my life."

— J.K. ROWLING

TIMING IS EVERYTHING

The average human has a hard time with the word patience. Raise your hand if you have a parent who has ever uttered the phrase, "Patience is a virtue." In other words, people who are patient are often considered to be of high moral standards, according to the dictionary definition of the word. In the click, click, buzz, buzz, now, now times in which we are living, it almost seems like patience is a long-forgotten relic. However, chances are that if you are reading this book, there has been at least one time in your life when you had to exercise patience. This could relate to finding the right job, the market viability for buying a home, or even when to start a romantic relationship. Not getting what we want, when we want it, can sometimes feel like the world is closing in.

Then, it happens, the perfect opportunity presents itself, and behold, our vision becomes 20/20, and we say things like, “That must have been a blessing in disguise” or “I’m so glad that last thing fell through.” What if we were able to fast forward to that attitude in the moment of disappointment, instead of at the time of hindsight, saying, “I guess that opportunity was not for me?” or “There must be something better on the horizon.” Wouldn’t we save ourselves so much heartache? I am not saying to skip the feelings of disappointment because those are valid and real, but if we could, after the loss, bounce back more quickly to the posture of belief that there is something better suited to us, how powerful that would be.

A good friend of mine waited a long time before she found her mate (I can literally write a whole book on this topic, but I’ll keep it brief). She was 35 years old, and up until that point had had several relationships, none of which resulted in marriage. Then a mysterious man rolled into town for a wedding that they both attended. They were instantly taken by each other, but there was one little issue: he was only 26 years old. There’s a lot that happens for a person developmentally and experientially in a decade. By this time in her life, she had graduated from college and had lived in numerous U.S. cities, in addition to living overseas, and he was literally just graduating from college. Overlooking this potential age hurdle, they moved forward with the relationship. Today they have been married for nearly 20 years, and have three children. There is no way the two of them could have gotten married when she originally wanted to, in her 20s, because he’d only been a teenager. She had to wait until the time was right, and it was worth the wait.

ONLY THE EVENT WILL TEACH US IN ITS HOUR

Two people in my life used to tell me, "Time will reveal all things," and "Only the event will teach us in its hour." For someone like me, whose inherent character flaw is impatience, these phrases challenged my very nature. I knew, however, that what they were saying was true. It was a matter of accepting and embracing it.

There is nothing in this life that promises we will know the exact process or outcome of anything. Essentially, there are no guarantees in life. You take a job, and are excited for your new journey, and it is quite possible that later down the line, the job you thought would be a dream has become a nightmare. There is no guarantee for relationships, either. We say "I do," and hope that we will live happily ever after, but we have no idea how things will turn out.

We often try to forecast how our lives will turn out. Here is one for example. I will go to college right after high school, spend four years studying the very thing I know I want to pursue, then just after graduation, I will land my dream job. At age 25, I'll be married, and by the time I'm 30 I'll have my third child. Does any of this sound familiar? Were these your life projections? Well, this is what I concocted in my 20-year-old mind. Let's look at the reality. I did go to college right after high school, but it took me six years to graduate, after having changed my major three or four times. Grad school was not a part of my projections, but the event taught me in its hour that I needed it to progress my career. I'd planned to go to grad school right after college graduation, but time revealed that I needed to take two years off to gain work experience, and to avoid scholastic burnout. With respect to the marriage projection, well, I'm still single as of writing this book, well into my 40s, and I have zero children.

Am I sad or bitter about the way my life has turned out? To be honest, I have struggled for many years about not having found my life partner, and in my early thirties, I came to the realization that I didn't want to have children after all. What I have experienced, however, during these years as a single person is having the freedom to start two businesses, the ability to publish a novel, the flexibility to start a second career path as a writer, and the privilege of visiting over 15 foreign countries.

My life has turned out nothing like my projections. I have received all the hindsight, insight, and wisdom that I could not have experienced without the passing of time. I am fulfilled, and can confidently and peacefully go into the unknown with open arms and unclenched fists because I realize that whatever the next event needs to teach me, I will be ready to receive it.

TIMES OF ADVERSITY

Hardships are inevitable. As individuals, we all experience our own personal pain, traumas, and challenges. If we allow them to do their work, they can help us become more authentic human beings. Struggles teach us to be more compassionate, thus giving us the ability to comfort others in their pain. Without adversity, we would be one-dimensional and unrelatable.

Just as individuals go through the process of refinement through the crucible of hardship, so do nations. I started writing this book in January of 2020, and who knew it would literally be one of the most trying times, not just for me, but for the entire planet. In my world, it started with the death of a well-known and beloved sports icon, Kobe Bryant. The city, the nation, and dare I say, the world lost one of the most prolific basketball players of our time. Adding insult to injury, not only was his wife left a widow, but she also lost a child. For months, my heart ached for her!

Fast forward a couple of months, and the world was learning about a new virus that began to sweep across the globe. COVID-19 changed the way we operated as a society, forcing us into our homes, distanced from the ones we love. For some, this created a sense of loneliness; for others, they were overwhelmed by how much time they now spent with families as homes became schools, offices, places of recreation, and child care, all in one. Millions of people lost jobs, lifelong businesses, and homes. Many felt a loss of the sense of freedom with the mandated stay-at-home orders. People lost friends and family members to the awful disease. Divorce and abuse rates rose, and people's mental health began to suffer as a result of prolonged isolation.

Only a short few months later, the world exploded as George Floyd was unjustly murdered at the hands of law enforcement, which catapulted the U.S. and the world into a social justice revolution of magnitudes we had not known since the 1960s. This all followed up with one of the most divisive times in American history, since the Civil War, as we experienced a polarizing political climate that continued to highlight the disparities and racism in the United States.

We can easily ask the question, "Why?" What is the point of all of this adversity? This is an age-old question to which I do not have the answer. However, there is not one person I have spoken to who has not been changed by the aforementioned events. Many expressed a renewed lease on life, a changed perspective, stronger relationships, or they realized during this time that they needed to change the way they moved through life, and even perhaps shed some relationships. Recently, I saw a quote on the marquis of a dry cleaners, *"Not all storms come to disrupt your life, some come to clear your path." Unknown.*

From the storms I have weathered in my life, I can confidently say that from them I have grown into the person I am today, and while bitterness has often knocked at my door, I have chosen instead to be better.

What storms have you weathered, and how have they shaped you, made you better, stronger, wiser or more compassionate?

RUNNING OUT OF TIME

Please allow me to be vulnerable for a moment. Not too long ago, I was talking with one of my aunts, who has also been a mentor over the years. She was helping me to understand some things that I was feeling, subconsciously. She called it the little girl that lives within. I was lamenting that I had to go back into the work world on a full-time basis because my business was not producing a profit. I was telling her that I was grateful to have the job, which provided a steady paycheck, but internally, I was very much struggling with the idea of working for someone again, especially since I had been working for myself for several years.

She kept redirecting me to understand my true feelings, which again, were on a subconscious level. While my head was saying, "Be grateful you have a job," my inner voice was screaming, "I feel trapped!" It took several rounds of back and forth until I finally broke down. Talking through tears, I blurted out, "I feel like I am running out of time!"

For much of my life, I have had the goal of starting a foundation that would provide funds to organizations that serve high-risk youth through the expressive arts and entrepreneurialism, and to use my wealth to do community development work overseas; for all of this, I had a specific age for which I'd hoped it would all be in place.

During the time of the conversation with my aunt, this was a mere six-and-a-half years away. It seemed like my plans were being derailed, and like I was going backwards in life. I had worked so hard, and for so many years on my business, only to see very little return on my investment. I felt stuck and duped. After having cried, and admitting to my TRUE feelings, I was able to then look at the notion of "Running out of time" more clearly. I had to ask myself, whose time was I on, really? I'm the one who set the parameters around when I thought these goals should be achieved. Why was I holding so tightly to this timeline, which, in actuality, I had no control over?

I started to call myself the frustrated entrepreneur because the need to take a full-time job in order to make ends meet, while trying to build a business (on the side), became very frustrating for me. Why couldn't I have it all? Run my business AND make a living. Then I came up with this phrase: "I long for the day that my passions and my paycheck intersect", and thus a prayer came to be, "Please allow my passions, skills, abilities, gifts, and talents all to be used for the sake of making a living."

Only a few months later, that very thing began to take shape. Currently, I am writing, decorating homes, and consulting - all things that I consider to be passions. The ability to be able to give my money on a grand scale is around the corner, and until then, I will make small strides at philanthropy through the giving of my time and energy to those who need it most. I will trust that my goals will happen when the time is right.

8

AGING, DEATH & DYING

"Time is long, but life is short."

— STEVIE WONDER

OUT WITH THE OLD, IN WITH THE NEW

In the Western World, the United States to be specific, we are not kind to the aging, nor to the aging process. The media has done a number on people's view of aging. As a whole, we look down on the aging - they're slow, wrinkled, and unsightly. As a society, we put these people away in homes and out of our minds. I have heard many people say, "I don't want to get old." My response is typically "Well, there is an alternative for that." While dying young is generally not something people want, it seems like we try at all costs to hold on to youth. With the era of plastic surgery, altering our looks to try and "remain young" is just at the fingertips of a doctor and a scalpel.

When did aging become synonymous with losing hope or becoming irrelevant? There was a time, in my recent past, that I began to realize I was the elder in the room. Being a Generation Xer, I have felt being eclipsed by the generations behind me, losing connection with pop culture, and no longer able to "compete" physically with 20 and 30-year-olds. I started to believe the lies of what has been sold to me by the media, marketing, and advertising, that older people are pariahs.

I have gained a new perspective on age, in general. In my mind, it is not that I am "older" than the 20 or 30-year-old. I've just been here (on Earth) longer. I was once in my 20s and 30s, and am nearing my fifth decade on this planet. This is not to say that I cannot learn something from a 20 or 30-year-old, or from a child, for that matter. However, I can honestly say there is not enough money that would make me want to go back to those times if it meant trading in the knowledge, wisdom, and lived experience that only comes with time. The confidence I now have to speak my mind, the lack of insecurity I have when walking into a room, and the comfort in knowing that whatever pain I may be experiencing will too pass, is priceless.

I'd like to address my younger folks for a moment. Be careful not to look at older people as obsolete because they have far surpassed where you currently are, which means they were once the "hot" person in the room. You might say, they don't understand me or my culture, but they too, have lived through not being understood by their elders. How is it that we could possibly think they have nothing to offer? They have lived through wars, heartbreaks, raised families, and had successful businesses. They have made it to the other side of any trauma or adversity life could throw at them, and God willing, you will also grow "old." At which point do you want to be disregarded and discarded? Or do you want someone to look at you and say, "Wow, I can learn a lot from her or him?" We need to honor our elders, and learn from their lived experience, and mistakes, gleaning whatever knowledge they have to offer because they have been there, done that.

Now to my contemporaries, and those who have gone before me. Why are we trying so hard to hold onto "youth." Remember the saying, "Youth is wasted on the young." Sure, we may not see the same youthful reflection in the mirror, but I want to encourage you not to buy into the lie that advertisers have told us for so long —that young is better. Growing old gracefully to me does not mean hiding the signs of aging through plastic surgery. Growing old gracefully to me means taking pleasure in all that I've learned over these past decades. It means accepting that my body cannot do the same things it once did, and being fine with that. It means accepting my limitations and being alright with modifying my physical activities in an effort to be kinder to my body. There is no need to compare myself to a 20-year-old. Of course, they move faster, are more limber, and have more physical endurance. One thing older adults have is mental and emotional endurance. We have had to push past hard times and overcome, which makes us perseverant.

There are many other societies that do not adopt the same Western notion of aging. Places like Italy, and many African, Asian, and Latin American countries, where people honor, respect, and even revere their elders. I would really love it if, as a society, we could look at it in this way.

THE DASH BETWEEN THE DATES

For some, this section may seem a smidge morbid, but what is life without thinking of our impending departure from this Earth. Have you ever thought about the small little dash mark between the birth and death date on a tombstone? This term, "the dash between the dates", was first made popular by the poem, *The Dash,* by Linda Ellis, and later inspired the book of the same name which she co-authored with Mac Anderson. The concept emphasizes the life we live is represented by the dash in between our birth date and death date. That little, seemingly insignificant line, is essentially the sum total of who we were, what we accomplished, who we affected, what we did and who we inspired while here on this planet.

As I acknowledge the reality of my limited time here, it helps to light a fire under me as I pursue my life's purposes. This knowledge also helps me to treat others better, and it helps the little life irritants roll off my back. It encourages me to be more grateful for what I have, rather than looking at the things I don't have, and it gives me the ability to choose my battles and let go of the small stuff. Once we are gone, we will not be remembered for all of our accomplishments or what we said, but rather, we will be remembered for how we treated people, how we made others feel, and the impact we made on them. On my proverbial tombstone, I simply want it to read, "She inspired me!" We all have a personal timeline. What do you want to be remembered for? What will you do with that dash between your dates?

TIME WAITS FOR NO ONE

I dare say humans are just as consumed with the issue of time, and how much of it we have, as we are about money. Each is fleeting, and each is necessary. The difference, however, between time and money is that with lost money you can make more, but with time you can never get back what you lose. The calendar will never read the same date twice, at least not ever the same month, day and year. We are focused on time because we know time is finite, limited and not promised. According to a variety of sources, the average lifespan of an American man ranges from 76-78 years for men and 78-81 years for women. If you are 20, this may seem like a long time off, but if you are 50, you are closing in on the understanding that time is of the essence.

Death has a way of reminding us that time is short and that it waits for no one, nor does it discriminate. Whether you are rich or poor, black or white, old or young, it will have the final say. The loss of a loved one is one of the single hardest things to wrap our minds around, and one of the most difficult experiences one can have.

My aunt Jean died at the age of 48. It was Memorial Day, 2001. She was on her way to a picnic with my oldest cousin and her four-year-old daughter. They were on Pear Blossom Highway in the high desert, just outside of the Palmdale/Lancaster area. Jean had just gotten her life on track after many years of dealing with addiction. In the early 1990s, she was diagnosed with HIV, and after losing her life partner to the disease, she did some incredible work to turn her life around. In fact, so much so that she was working at the Employment Development Department, helping people to find jobs. I was a recent college graduate and was having a hard time finding a job myself, so she offered to meet with me on the Tuesday after Memorial day. The plan was to drive out from Torrance to her office in the Antelope Valley. I was grateful for the help, but mostly excited that she was the one helping me.

Unbeknownst to me, that meeting would never happen. I was at another aunt's house when my mother called. For whatever reason, I chose not to answer the call and decided I'd call her on my way to my next appointment. Here is how the phone call went:

Mother: Jennifer, Isa, Jean, and Zena were in a car accident.
Me: (Silence, as my heart plummeted with the thought of - "Which one of them died?")
Mother: Jean died.
Me: Are you serious?
Mother: Would I joke about something like that?

The next thing I knew, I was doubled over on the sidewalk, wailing at the top of my lungs. I had to quickly pull myself together, just enough to go back into my aunt's house, where I handed her the phone so that my mother could repeat the news. Now, my aunt and cousin were both sobbing uncontrollably. I watched in pain at their response. My cousin had a two-year-old daughter who was witnessing all of this, and I felt I needed to hold it together for her.

Now, over 25 years later, Jean's death still remains one of the most difficult life events I have ever had to endure.

Death is imminent, and as my aunt Sheila has so eloquently stated, on numerous occasions, none of us will leave this place alive. To those who don't like thinking about death, and may have never experienced loss, it may be unbearable to imagine.

You may have heard the saying, live each day as if it were your last. I have often had a hard time subscribing to this because it seems exhausting. If I were to live a day like it was my last, it would look a lot like this: I'd pull out all the money in my savings and checking accounts, go on a shopping spree, and buy things for the people I was about to leave behind; or simply withdraw the cash and distribute to my family. I'd eat creme brulee for breakfast, a hamburger, french fries, mac and cheese for lunch and follow it up with a double scoop of banana ice cream. For dinner, I'd gorge myself on sushi, Mexican, and Indian food, and by the end of the day, I'd be broke, jobless, and most likely have a raging case of indigestion.

Instead of living each day like it was my last, I choose to treat each 24 hours with the utmost respect. I do my best to be as productive as possible without burning myself out. I try my hardest to treat people the way I would want to be treated. I make it my aim to laugh, smile, and count the many, many blessings in my life. Even if on some days I feel like I'd rather give up, I do my best to remember to be thankful. I thank my God for each of those years I have already received. I'm thankful for the good days, bad days, the highest highs, and the lowest lows. I'm thankful because I am still among the living, and I still have a voice and a chance to make a difference in this world.

So what will it be? How will you spend your 24 hours? Will you spend it berating the driver who is going too slowly, will you spend it yelling at your employees, kids, or the neighbor whose music is playing too loudly? Will you spend it fretting over things for which you have no control, or being so caught up in the future that you cannot see the blessings that are right in front of you? Or will you spend it reaching for your goals, loving those around you, and making the most of each day that you are given? Life is short (cliché maybe, but true) and none of us is guaranteed another day, week, month or year. I hardly imagine that my aunt Jean thought on her way to the picnic that it would be her last day on this planet.

Be careful not to put things off for when you're older, have more money, you get "settled", married, have a better job, more time, etc., etc., etc. You are not guaranteed to be married, settled, rich or otherwise "ready" to take that plunge, so what are you waiting for? Don't wait for the perfect weight or the perfect mate, live your best life now!

Principle #2 Summary

- Whether or not we'd like to admit it, there is not much we can control in life - including other people, the passage of time, or the length of time we have on this planet.
- Holding too tightly to outcomes creates in us a need for control, which inevitably creates stress for ourselves and those around us.
- Coming to terms with, and accepting the fact that much of life is out of our control, we will hopefully become more filled with peace, surrender, and grace for ourselves and others.
- What we *can* control is our attitude, our behaviors, and our outputs.

Putting Principle #2 Into Practice

1. What are some areas/events/opportunities in your life that you can look back on and admit you are glad they didn't happen when you had hoped? Why?
2. When dealing with life pauses and times of hardship, do you more often feel frustrated or angry, or do you understand that this is a necessary time of growth? If the former, what are some ways you can work on shifting your mindset?
3. How do you view aging? Is it something that you dread, or is it something you accept as an inevitable part of life? Are you trying to hang on to youth, or are you accepting of the limitations that come with age?
4. How do you want to be remembered in this life? If you could put a phrase on your headstone, what would it be?
5. Knowing the inevitability of your own mortality, what are the areas of your life/goals you plan to focus more on?

Challenge: The next time you are tempted to become impatient with life or an endeavor, pause, try asking the question, "What am I supposed to be learning during this time?"

PRINCIPLE #3: EFFECTIVELY PRIORITIZING, ORGANIZING & MANAGING YOUR TIME

"Day, n. A period of twenty-four hours, mostly misspent."

— AMBROSE BIERCE

Have you ever wondered why some people are so productive? Do you ever struggle with reaching your goals? Have you ever found yourself saying, "If only I had more time?" Productive people do not have more time; they have the same 24 hours in a day as the next person. They also are not superheroes; they simply prioritize what's important to them and focus on those goals until they are reached.

Having a clear view of what it is you want out of life, what's valuable to you, your "why," will help you to more readily reach your goals. Once you have effectively identified your purpose and vision, then you can best find a system of organization that best works for you.

In this section, we will discuss the importance of prioritizing, effectively planning, organizing, and managing your time. We will identify ways in which you may be robbing yourself of time and ways to maximize your usage of time. Finally, we will uncover the systems, tactics, and time management tools that have proven to be most effective in my personal and professional life.

9
PRIORITIZING YOUR TIME

"Things which matter most, must never be at the mercy of things that matter least."

— JOHANN WOLFGANG VON GOETHE

When we know our priorities, we can better utilize our time. We hear the term priorities thrown around a lot, but what does that really mean to you? If everything were a priority, to-do lists would be incredibly long. There are numerous time management experts, including David Allen, author of *Getting Things Done*, who initiate the conversation by defining your priorities. In Stephen Covey *The 7 Habits of Highly Effective People,* Principle 3 - "Putting first things First," he asserts that we need to "Organize and execute around priorities." As defined by Dictionary.com, priority means the fact or condition of being regarded or treated as more important. It's hard to put first things first if we do not know what those first things are.

Have you ever had a weekend day that went awry? You were in the middle of washing dishes, you received some unplanned phone calls which cost you about 45 minutes. After that distraction, you realized you had forgotten to pick up an item and had to go back to the store. Then, you saw a squirrel and sat, daydreaming about how much easier your life would be if you were one. Once you came back to consciousness, you realized it was time to pick up your kid from karate class and start dinner. By the time your day was over you felt as much like a chaotic mess as your day was. If we are not careful we can go through life being tossed by the wind and the waves of distractions, those pesky "urgent" matters that often get in the way of what we truly value. Without setting the intention of putting ourselves back on the course of our priorities, it will be easy to never fully achieve, never fully arrive or never fully actualize that which we most value.

What is most important to you? Is it your family and friends, your mental or physical health, traveling? Just like how we spend money on what is important to us, we also need to spend our time on what is important to us. I have said *no* to many, many invitations and opportunities because it simply did not fit within my priorities. I, like many before me, believe wholeheartedly that we cannot even begin the conversation about time management without first identifying our priorities.

DEFINING YOUR VALUES

It is much easier to prioritize our time when we know what our values are. I once took a two-day workshop, called *"Discover your Core Values"* created by Amy Johnson. The purpose of the workshop was to help identify, define, and elaborate one's core values. Dictionary.com defines values as the attitudes, behaviors, and social structures toward which the people of a society or group have a deeply ingrained, positive or negative emotional regard.

Whether or not we are fully aware, these ideals are generally the guiding light to the decisions we make in our lives, the way we spend our time, with whom we spend our time, and what we choose to pursue. Our values can often be in our subconscious mind, so putting a name to them is quite helpful. After I went through the process, I left with a very full understanding of my seven core values. It was the first time in my life that I had actually named and defined them. At the same time, it completely made sense, as I felt like I had been living according to these values for much of my life. My values are as follows: *Humanity, Communication, Beauty & Nature, Health & Wellness, Purpose, Creativity, and Experiences. Humanity* was in perfect alignment with my chosen profession as a social worker and my love of other people's cultures. Communication is directly linked to my love of words, writing, and conveying clear messages to those around me. *Creativity* plays a role in my life in so many areas, from writing to interior design, marketing to cooking, photography, and dancing, just to name a few. I recently started making my own skin care products to avoid harsh chemicals, and whenever possible, I choose a homeopathic means for healing small ailments, aligning with *Health & Wellness.* When I exercise, I try to ensure that at least one or more of those days are outdoors so that I can enjoy *Beauty & Nature.* I love to travel, and it is my goal to do so at least once per year in an effort to continue to gather life *Experiences.*

Discovering your values can save precious time on your path to discovering and living out your most meaningful life. In addition, it can help you whittle away the areas of your life that may feel like dead weight and are essentially not adding any worth. At this stage in my life, I have decided that I only want to engage in activities and pursuits that align with my priorities and values.

ASK YOURSELF THIS QUESTION

As you continue to determine what is important, you will begin to fully grasp what it is you should be doing with your time, and whether or not the time you use is going to get you to your goal.

Understand that in no way am I saying that everything we do has to revolve around goals. Life is not simply about achievement. There is a time for work and a time for play, and in order to be truly fulfilled in this life, we must have balance. What I am saying is that when you are going after a goal, you need to be hyper-focused on it, more than other lesser areas of your life. That being said, you need to ask yourself when you get sucked into social media feeds, find yourself putting out urgent, but non-important fires, TV binging for hours on end, or any other number of time sucking activities, "Is this the best use of my time?

I imagine that even before you ask the question, you will know the answer, but ask it anyway. This will alert you and hopefully get you back on track.

URGENT, IMPORTANT OR NONE OF THE ABOVE

Have you ever felt like a scatter-brain? Going with the wind of chaos to wherever you allow it to take you. Juggling any number of items on your to-do list with no real sense of purpose or structure.

Much of the time when someone (especially a boss) asks us to do something, it can be interpreted as, or truly is, an urgent matter. However, it is a very good practice to ask your supervisor where this task lies in the area of priority.

I took a one-day time management seminar very early in my professional life. It was highlighting Author Stephen Covey's quadrant system, made widely known through his book *The 7 Habits of Highly*

Effective People. After learning these principles, my life has never looked the same. These principles have guided me in effectively navigating my calendar, my day, and even other peoples' requests.

The system is based on four categories of tasks and their order of importance, including: urgent, important, not urgent, and not important. Covey further details the system, which is defined by the pairing of each one of the quadrants, with the other: ***Urgent & Important*** = Crises, pressing problems, deadline-driven project; ***Urgent & Not Important*** = Interruptions, certain incoming calls, certain mail, some reports, certain meetings. ***Not Urgent & Important*** = Prevention, capability improvement, relationship building, new opportunities, planning, recreation. ***Not Urgent & Not Important*** = Trivia, busy work, some mail, some phone calls, time wasters, pleasant activities.

These principles, if applied effectively, can help you avoid constantly running around, putting out other people's or even your own urgent, but not important, fires.

DON'T MINIMIZE PERSONAL DEADLINES

While our work priorities are easily divided into the urgent, important, not urgent, not important, it is not so cut and dried when it comes to our personal lives. In the work or business environment, we have deadlines constantly imposed upon us. We must meet them for the security of our jobs or to keep our business afloat. For example, creating monthly reports, reaching sales goals, or hiring new staff.

Outside of work, we often have personal goals, projects we want to complete or challenges we need to conquer. Maybe your goal is to hike the highest mountain, knit a sweater, or cook some new recipes. Sometimes, when it comes to our personal goals, we can tend to put them on the back burner because more pressing issues, like work or family, take center stage. I believe that personal goals, while generally not urgent, are very important. Thus, it is a good idea to put deadlines on our individual endeavors as well. While the deadlines we impose on ourselves are more flexible than work deadlines, in the end, creating target dates can help you reach your objective, and that always feels good.

I DON'T HAVE TIME FOR THAT

Some of us genuinely cannot add one more to-do list item to our plate, so this section may not apply to you. For years and years, I have said to a family member, after they made the statement, "That costs money." My rebuttal, "Everything costs money; it just depends on what you want to spend it on."

For instance, I am very frugal when it comes to things like clothing, shoes, and other material goods. So much so there was a time in my life that I would shop second-hand for clothes and household items. However, since I value experiences over material possessions, I can easily drop thousands of dollars on travel without even blinking.

Much like how we spend money on what we value, the same is true for how we spend our time. Thus, someone who says, "I don't have time to...workout, volunteer, read, learn that new skill," is most likely saying, "My time is valuable to me, and those things just aren't that important."

10
TIME MANAGEMENT 101

"You may delay, but time will not."

— BENJAMIN FRANKLIN

There are hundreds, if not thousands of books and theories on time management. Some of those trusted, and widely known methods include greats like David Allen, the author of *Getting Things Done*. In his methodology, he discusses the four D's: Do it right away, Delegate, Defer, and Delete, which are similar to Stephen Covey's time management matrix of urgent and important, which we discussed earlier. Allen also emphasizes the importance of writing things down to get them out of your head, creating project lists by category, removing clutter from your space, and emphasizes focusing on one task at a time, all of which I wholeheartedly agree with. In addition, he states that people are able to accomplish more when there are no open loops or undone commitments floating around in their mind.

The authors of *The 12 Week Year,* Brian P. Moran and Michael Lennington emphasize that since people are prone to procrastinate, tending to take a last quarter approach by cramming all of their goals into the last three months of the year, that they should use that same approach throughout the year, essentially tricking the brain by creating a sense of urgency in which they have a shorter segments of time to complete projects.

Moran and Lennington also assert that we need to designate blocks of time within our day, creating order and efficiency. These blocks include "Strategic Blocks" for focused work, "Breakout Blocks" for times of rest, and "Buffer Blocks," times in which we give ourselves padding in our schedule to account for unexpected events.

While I will be sharing some of the ways I most effectively manage my own time, I believe time management implementation is based upon personal preference. Time management, in my opinion, is half methods and tactics, and half mindset. Once we have developed a conviction about our dreams, goals, values and priorities, it is then up to us to choose the tactical time management system that works best for us.

In the following pages, I will share with you some of the technical and tactical ways in which I manage my time.

ONE DAY AT A TIME

A big goal can be overwhelming when you are just starting out. I have known people who feel paralyzed when they have a lot to do, and sometimes respond by doing nothing. Sometimes, looking at your timeline, to-do list, or the end goal can feel like an ocean of impossibility. We've heard the saying, "You can't see the forest for the trees", which essentially means that we get stuck on the minuscule details, and can't see the big picture, but now I am giving you permission to do the opposite. Don't look at the forest in this instance; it is too big, too overwhelming. Start by looking at one tree. Then look at the next tree, and so on, until you reach your goal.

In the past, I would look at my calendar incessantly, sometimes every hour, and while planning, for me, is a very peaceful practice I was finding myself overwhelmed. The futurist in me would look at weeks and months ahead, feeling pressured and stressed by all I had to undertake.

I finally had a conversation with myself that went like this, "Jennifer, why are you looking at March when February just started?" Time management has as much to do with mindset as it does with tactics. When I was able to let go of the perceived control, and come to terms with the fact that no matter how much planning I actually did, I truly have no power or control over future life events. Once I was able to admit this, I began to feel a real sense of peace, and the stress began to wane.

It was then, and only then, that I was able to focus on one day at a time. Sometimes even one hour at a time.

Don't underestimate or downplay the impact of incremental accomplishments. When I was using a weight-loss method several years ago, called *Body for Life,* in the beginning, it felt daunting. How in the world was I supposed to reach this goal in the 12-week period they said it would take. Every day I would simply tell myself, "One day at a time." I could only control what I ate and the workouts I did, one day at a time. When I did this, I did not overwhelm myself by thinking about the 12 weeks ahead of me, and by the time I looked up I had reached, and even exceeded, my goal.

Maybe your goal this year is to read more, but you think to yourself, how in the world am I going to get through even one book, let alone five. Let's look at this in the model of one day at a time. If for example, you read five pages per day for the entire year, by the end of the year, you'll have read 1,825 pages. Broken down even further, this would be seven, 250-page books.

Suppose you have a room that needs to be organized, but it feels insurmountable. Section off the room into areas (i.e. closet, under the bed, etc.). The one day at a time method would look something like this: Monday, you clean under the bed, Tuesday, you clean out the closet, Wednesday, you go through any paperwork or photo albums that need organizing, Thursday, you wipe down the walls, and so on. If you get tired, overwhelmed or bored, take a break, walk away and get back to it later. Each completed project is a small victory; remember to celebrate those. By the end of the week, you will have an organized room or will be that much closer to your end goal.

Part of my time writing this book was when I was working a retail job for about a year and a half. In that world taking a lunch break is a requirement. I'd bring my computer to work, and even for just 20 minutes, would write. My bosses marveled at what they called 'my discipline.' Those twenty minutes a day, 4 - 5 days a week, added up to the completion of this book.

I cannot stress enough the fact that the minutes and hours add up, and those minutes and hours make the sum total of your daily choices, decisions, actions, and outcomes.

You are the captain of your dreams and goals. The only person you have to answer to is you, so be kind, flexible, and gracious with yourself. No judgments needed. If you did not accomplish those items in that particular day or week, simply move them the next. My timeline and calendar is always written in pencil, for this very reason. If you don't meet a deadline, there's tomorrow.

WIGGLE ROOM

Most of us wear a number of hats: parent, employee, volunteer, church goer, sports mom or dad, and with this comes back to back meetings, events and obligations.

As we know, I have certainly been guilty of this, and is the very crux of the running joke my aunts had about how I used to schedule my days. They'd say "If you want an appointment with Jennifer, she will be available between 12:15 p.m. and 12:22 p.m.." I lived this way well into my 20s, with college, back-to-back meetings, appointments, classes, working, and exercise. Allowing myself no downtime, no room for time errors, no room to rest or to simply live. Although I was a young person doing this, and had the required physical endurance, no matter what your age, this is not a healthy way to be. Even if your body can keep up, your mind and your psyche will eventually burn out.

Fortunately, as I have matured, I have learned the art and science of being fully productive, fully present, and fully in control of my time. While I still have plenty on my calendar, most days I try not to have much more than four major items that I need to accomplish. When I say major, I mean more than a quick phone call or online bill pay.

Wiggle room also allows for the necessary time for transitions in between projects and meetings or to take time to recuperate, reset your mind, your intentions or simply just to veg out.

There are no hard and fast rules for any of this, which is where the art of it comes in, and you know your limits. Giving yourself some wiggle room allows for time to breathe in between your projects (even if it's only 15 minutes), and to be able to manage the unexpected. Whether you simply take a break to breathe, watch the sunset, stretch, eat a healthy meal, reflect, lounge for a bit, allow for the time to do so.

TIMES OF TRANSITION

We just briefly touched upon the inevitable transitions that take place throughout our day, allowing time to get from appointment to appointment. Then there are transitions that come in the form of significant life markers, like changing jobs, moving homes, getting married, or becoming a parent.

Transitions can be volatile and unpredictable, much like that of winter turning to spring - one day it's freezing cold and the next it's warm and sunny. Life transitions, if we are not careful, can be cause for serious stress, depending on how we view them and move through them. I have found that during these times of uncertainty is when I am the most tested in my contentment, patience, and trust.

Times of transition can also be messy. Let's look at moving to a new home as an example. During this time, your current home is in full disarray and filled with boxes. You must juggle renting a truck, changing your mailing address, enlisting the help of movers, not to mention all the other daily life commitments such as school and work. During moves, you are often left without your creature comforts, like dishes and utensils, so now you're eating off paper and plastic. It's quite likely you can't find many items you use on a daily basis, and you may very well be using a packing box as a dining table. It's hectic and chaotic and you quite likely feel anxious about the process, but without the mess you would not be able to get to your end goal, a new home.

While these times often feel like an abyss of ambiguity or a vacuum of wasted space, I have learned that it is during these periods in my life that I am the most reflective. Looking back on what once was, and pondering areas where I can grow as a result of an ending relationship or job.

Times of transition have also been a time when I can celebrate, with gratitude, the friendships, experiences, and circumstances that I am transitioning from.

Lastly, times of transitions can offer a moment to regroup, strengthen, and sometimes reinvent ourselves, all while anticipating the journey ahead.

When it is all said and done, times of transition are necessary to get us from where we currently are to where we desire to be. While these times inevitably bring about uncertainty and what feels like disorder, we will do ourselves a huge favor when we let go of trying to control the process, but rather breathe through the uncertainty, and ride the wave that will bring the desired tides of change.

See graph below for a visual representation of transitions.

TRANSITIONS

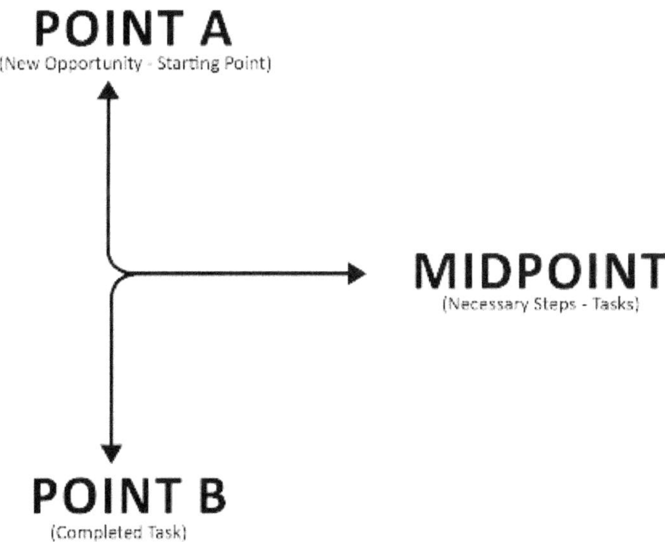

SEIZE THE DAY

Why put off tomorrow what you can do today? It's an age old saying, with so much wisdom. "I'll get around to that, some day." " I'll do that next week." However, next week never comes. Have no fear, you are not alone. Studies suggest that procrastination chronically affects around 15 to 20 percent of adults.

Research has also found that there are several factors that contribute to procrastination, and none of them is attributed to laziness. Some factors include certain personality traits like impulsivity and self-efficacy. Decision-making styles can be another factor, along with time perspectives, emotional regulation, and even biological factors, that come into play. Meaning, the majority of us procrastinate because we are biologically wired to, and once the temptation to procrastinate sets in, anything is more interesting than the task at hand.

The limbic system in our brain is responsible for emotion and behavior. It's a system of structures responsible for memory. One of the system's tasks is to stop you from doing unpleasant things. Touching the blade of a knife, for instance, would ignite a response in the limbic system to stop the behavior. This same system also tries to help you avoid things you don't want to do – like studying or working.

The prefrontal cortex, on the other hand, is responsible for processing information and making decisions. Basically, it's in charge of the thoughts and actions you take to reach a goal. The prefrontal cortex, however, requires you to consciously engage it. When you think "I should start my task", and you begin to kick into gear, the pesky limbic system is waiting in the wings to take over as soon as you disengage from your task.

When you start to get distracted from an unpleasant task, the limbic system starts a process called 'immediate mood repair.'

Doing a more pleasant task provides the brain with a small amount of dopamine, which is the chemical in the brain that controls our pleasure and reward centers. If you do or see something good, you'll get a little hit of dopamine. Your brain likes this, and you'll be more likely to keep doing whatever it is that releases the dopamine. In the case of procrastination, you're being rewarded for not doing the task that you're supposed to do because it feels better for your brain.

There are several different types of people who procrastinate. Researchers have separated them into two categories: passive procrastinators - people who delay tasks because they struggle to make decisions and act on them, and active procrastinators - those who purposefully delay tasks because they feel they work better under pressure.

Other such categories include "The worrier" - people who put things off because they worry about the challenge or about leaving their comfort zone. "The overdoer" - someone that often takes on too much and then struggles to find the time to complete everything. "The perfectionist" avoids tasks because they doubt their ability to complete them perfectly. Someone who may be considered a "dreamer" might put off tasks because they're potentially not good at focusing on the details. "The defier" is someone who dislikes someone dictating their schedule, and "the crisis-maker" puts off tasks because they prefer working under the pressure of tight deadlines.

While it's true that some of us are more predisposed to procrastinating than others, it's possible to train your brain to reduce how often you do it. Much of this involves thinking about the future to imagine how good it would feel to finish the task, or how bad it would be if you don't get it done in time. Think of it as trading some small dopamine hits for a much bigger one at the end. The next time you find yourself procrastinating on the things that you know are good for you, think about the lasting feeling of bliss and accomplishment you'll have if you actually complete them, rather than the temporary one you'll receive for putting it off.

THE GET 'ER DONE CONTINUUM

An accomplished goal or dream is birthed through a combination of working, and waiting, and working, and hoping, and working, and wanting to give up, but not. The key ingredient is action. No dream, unless the ones that happen in our sleep, happens overnight or without a little blood, sweat, and tears. The difference between people who dream and never accomplish anything, and those who actually do, is in the "doing."

We don't generally think of a continuum when we think of getting things done. Most of us think of a checklist. However, we are going to approach it from a philosophical perspective, and once again, examine ourselves to understand where we fall on this continuum of "doing."

With any spectrum or continuum, there are polar opposites, and most of the time being on either side of the poll can be a place of extremism. In order to be successful, we must do our best to avoid extremes and find a balance. We are first going to look at two extremes on the *Get-er Done Continuum* (See graph below).

THE GET'ER DONE CONTINUUM

Paralysis of Analysis (Paralyzed)

If you have been alive for at least the past several decades, you may well remember an advertising campaign launched by Nike in the late 80's. The slogan was so popular that it still finds its way into conversations to this day. It's short, but so incredibly powerful. It essentially says don't make excuses, don't put it off for another day, don't talk about it, analyze it, make forecasts about it, "Just DO it!"

We all know someone, and maybe that someone is us, who talks about what they hope to achieve, someone who takes a long time to make decisions, feeling the need to talk through and pick apart every aspect, so much so that they never actually make a move. They ponder every effort and get stuck in indecision. Their process often goes beyond simply thinking through the process, and they can easily get stuck in philosophy, unwrapping every possibility, perceived risk or potential outcome. They talk about what they hope to accomplish one day, but can probably find multiple reasons why it won't work. The person paralyzed by their own analysis is often self-sabotaging, and quite possibly looking for ways to avoid having to do the very thing they know they should or could do. It becomes much easier to come up with reasons why they cannot, rather than facing the real issue, which is generally based in some type of fear, that of failure, or worse, the fear of success.

Disadvantages of Over Analysis

- Think too long before action, which can cause inaction
- Constantly staying in a place of theory/philosophy versus action - goals stay in the ideas phase
- Rarely achieve goals

Ways an Analyzer can turn Process into Progress

If you find it hard being motivated to "do," start with setting aside some time throughout the day. Whether it is five minutes or fifty, build the habit of doing at least something on a daily basis. This can be as simple as making a to-do list and aiming to get started on or even finishing one item on that list per day. It's like saving money, if you want to save, even putting aside $50 per month will get you $600 by the end of the year, and $600 is better than $0. Same is true with your goals; the more time you spend the closer you will get to the finish line. Most of us can find at least one hour out of our day. After you have done this, you will have spent up to 30 hours per month toward your goal. Here are some ways to get your engine started:

- Be realistic in your goal setting (using the SMART goal setting method, choosing goals that are Specific, Measurable, Attainable, Relevant/Realistic, and Time-Bound).
- Choose an accountability partner. If you have someone who you know will ask you how it's going you will be much more motivated to chip away at your to-do list.
- Work in increments of time, even if your hour is split up, it's still an hour (i.e. two 30-minute sessions or four 15-minute segments).
- Be kind to yourself. If you miss a day or two, just start fresh the next day. Don't spend time judging yourself or beating yourself up about it.
- Ask yourself the deeper "why" questions when you start to feel unmotivated (e.g. "Why am I so unmotivated right now?"). Once you understand the *why* you can tackle the *what.*

The Quick Start

We just discussed the person who rarely achieves goals because they are in a constant state of analysis. On the complete opposite end of that spectrum is the quick start. This person is a rapid fire of ideas, and action is their game. They are in a constant state of dreaming up new notions, ideas, and concepts. The issue with this, however, is that this person does not look before they leap. Instead, they jump in, head first, with little thought of consequence.

As someone who has experienced this type of boss on at least two occasions, I can confidently say that this type of behavior caused a real sense of chaos, anxiety, and feelings of uncertainty. When being led by this person, our team never successfully settled into any consistent processes or gained a real footing on implementation of these new ideas because we were in a constant state of change. Imagine moving into a new home, and before you can fully unpack, and make your bed you have to move again.

As a planner, this drove me nuts. In the midst of my workday, it was not uncommon for me to feel nervous because I was afraid some new, and inevitably "more urgent" project would arise, thus causing me to change course on my entire day, week or even month.

Disadvantages of the Quick Start

- Making costly mistakes (monetarily or reputation-wise)
- Driving people crazy
- Appearing wishy-washy
- Not taking people's time into account
- Being in a constant state of disorganization and disarray
- Losing people's respect and trust

Ways a Quick Start can Successfully Make the Magic Happen

Much of the time the quick start is someone who has lots of incredible ideas, however, it is often hard for them to find ways to implement those ideas. Here are some ways to turn those ideas into reality.

- Stop and think through all of the tools, resources, and capital you may need to embark on your new endeavor.
- Ask people who may have gone before you, in order to gain much-needed advice.
- Make a realistic timeline of how long you think this new project may take. If this is not your strong suit, ask for help.
- Make a realistic budget for how much you may need to spend on this endeavor.
- Find people who are willing to help you implement your idea.

Again, with anything in life, there needs to be balance. If we err on the side of overcautiousness, we can easily see life pass us by without ever achieving a thing. On the flip side, if we take action too quickly with little to no thought, it can result in sloppy outcomes that cause stress and can create a need for cleaning up what was started in haste. At the end of the day, we need to avoid overthinking to the point of inaction or not thinking things through at all.

"Do-ers" versus "Be-ers"

These are the people in the middle of the *Get 'er Done Spectrum*. You may identify either with a "do-er" (goal-focused) or a "be-er" (process-oriented) or a combination of the two. We may also know these two personality types as Type A or Type B. Keep in mind it is rare to be all or nothing within any spectrum, but it is most certainly possible to lean more to one of these than the other.

The do-er is someone who gains great satisfaction from getting things done, checking off lists, and accomplishing goals. They are focused on outcomes. The more they accomplish the more invigorated they feel. Be-ers are more inclined to enjoy the process it takes to reach an outcome. They relish more in all the steps it takes on the way to their goal than the end product.

Let's look at a do-er and a be-er at a hypothetical house party they planned and hosted together. For the do-er it is hard to even sit down at the party because they are so busy doing things like ensuring the buffet table looks good, cleaning up after people, rearranging the flowers, or asking people if they need another drink. They rarely take a breath or a moment to stop and have a sip of their own wine or even taste the deliciously catered food. After the party is over you better believe they are cleaning it all up. By the time they go to bed they have a satisfactory exhaustion that they successfully pulled off the party.

The be-er, on the other hand, is the person at the party who is working the room, connecting, talking, enjoying a plate of food, and some good wine. They may see the do-er running around, and to them it looks like pure chaos. They simply want to be at the party and feel the sense of enjoyment that comes with that.

During the planning of the party there may have been some friction because the do-er came armed with their to-do list, and the be-er quite likely was more concerned with who may show up, and how much fun it will be. The be-er was probably overwhelmed by the do-er's intensity level, and the do-er may have been frustrated at the be-er's relaxed approach.

Both personality types have their core strengths, and of course, with any strength comes drawbacks. The pitfalls of being a do-er is that it is easy to turn your interactions into transactions, missing the relational piece of the process. As a do-er myself, this is something I am constantly cognizant of, and have to ensure that I don't miss the human element of my dealings. On the flip side, a be-er can easily become more content in the moment, and working in the process that they may find it hard to actually finish projects or reach goals.

As a do-er it is a good idea to stop for a moment and join the proverbial party (life). Take a few moments to chit chat with your guests (the people in your life), have a sip of wine, take a bite, and enjoy the fruits of your labor.

For be-ers you may want to set timelines and deadlines for yourself to ensure the completion of your goals. Perhaps appoint an accountability partner who will help motivate you to reach the finish line.

YOU WANT SOMETHING DONE, GIVE IT TO THE BUSIEST PERSON YOU KNOW

When I first heard the quote, "If you want something done, give it to the busiest person you know," I thought that was the most ridiculous thing. I didn't fully comprehend it, until I understood Newton's first law of motion, often referred to as the law of inertia, which states that an object at rest stays at rest, and an object in motion stays in motion with the same speed and in the same direction unless acted upon by an unbalanced force.

In essence, if we are moving, it is hard to stop, and if we are stopped, it is hard to get moving. A moving freight train traveling 55 miles an hour can take nearly a mile to stop. The converse is true. Have you ever seen how long it takes a freight train to start moving from a dead stop. It's a painfully arthritic effort.

Humans are not much different from freight trains (chug-a, chug-a choo-choo)! When you are in the middle of a project, sometimes it's hard to stop because you're in motion, on a roll, in the flow.

The opposite is also true. Ever been at work, and there's a lull in time? Perhaps you have finished a project, and now have some down time, so you start to look at your social media feeds. You go on to daydream about what you will do over the weekend, and browse sites about your dream vacation. Then, wham, up walks a colleague or your boss, asking if you're working on something because they need your help. Starting a new project is the last thing you want to do, and let's be honest, you're really annoyed because now you have to rev up that cold engine.

Many moons ago, I worked for a very busy doctor and his family. He was the head of surgery, an elder in my church, in charge of a specialized ministry, had a wife and three very active teen daughters. I always marveled at how quickly he responded to my emails and text messages; literally, within 24 hours I would have a response. He was in a constant state of motion, and for that reason, he was able to achieve so much!

You may be thinking, but if I ask my busy friend to do something for me I'd be piling more on their plate, and could overwhelm them. This is a valid concern, and could very well be the case. However, the main point I'm making is the difference between asking someone who is busy, versus someone who has nothing going on to do something for you. While it would make complete sense that the person with little on their plate should be more than available, there is a reason they have little going on, and quite honestly, they might want to keep it that way. They are in that comfy place, the freight at a standstill, and the effort it would take to start the ignition, warm up the engine, and be ready to announce, "All Aboard" is more than a notion.

HIRING OTHERS SO YOU CAN FOCUS ON YOUR GENIUS

In Jack Canfield's book, *The Success Principles: How to Get from Where You Are to Where You Want to Be* - Principle #39, he discusses the notion of focusing on your core genius. This principle is also beautifully reiterated in Rachel Rodger's book, *We Should All Be Millionaires*, in the chapter entitled "Million Dollar Team." The crux of this principle is essentially that we should focus on what we are innately good at, that which comes with little to no effort - your gift, talent or what Canfield calls your genius. Some people believe that their genius is the thing they are supposed to be doing on this earth, and some of us are fortunate enough to be able to focus solely on our genius because it is also what pays the bills. Most of us, however, likely have a job that pays the bills and a genius that is being nurtured or ignored.

Canfield and Rodgers are both addressing people who want to achieve success. In that case, in order to focus on it means we cannot get caught in the weeds of lower-level tasks. Hear me that I am in no way saying lower in a derogatory sense, but rather lower in importance to our genius. It is also not about shirking your life responsibilities, but rather, optimizing your time (which we all know is a currency).

Essentially, if you have the means to hire out various tasks that would ordinarily take you away from your genius, then do so. For instance, in your personal life, you may have to juggle a nine-to-five, in addition to managing your home by way of cleaning and cooking. Can you afford to hire out some of the cleaning and cooking in an effort to save yourself the time to focus on your genius?

Perhaps you run a business, and like many entrepreneurs, we are the CEO and the janitor of our enterprise until we can get to a place financially where we can hire a team. Canfield stresses that we need to hire the people to do the tasks that get in the way of focusing on our genius. He suggests delegating completely, meaning assigning this new person the ownership of that said task. This means setting them up to be successful and essentially getting out of their way. This can be as big as hiring someone to manage your company's finances, and as small as hiring someone who can run errands for you. *Side note:* the personal assistant business is booming. In addition, when you focus on your genius, you are in turn focusing on that thing you are uniquely good at, your gift to the world.

I'll give you an example with my business owner hat on. I love graphic design. I'm good at conceptualizing logos, choosing fonts, laying out brochures, and postcards. Sometimes in my business I choose to spend time on this because it is something that brings me joy. However, when it comes to making a professional logo, I hire a graphic designer. Could I learn a program like InDesign or Photoshop? Yes, but how much time and effort would that take? Not to mention I would have to pay for the program, and the training on how to use it. I am not striving to become a professional graphic designer, so why not pay someone who already has the necessary programs and skills to do so, and who would have it done in a fraction of the time. While doing the task myself may save money, it will not save me time. I suppose if this were a book on saving money I may say something different, but alas, it is not.

Disclaimer: A little bit about what delegation is not. I once worked for a woman who hired out every aspect of her business. She delegated completely so as to focus on her genius. However, her downfall was that she knew very little about the operations of her company. Not only did she not know, but she seemed not to want to know. This caused her to seem incompetent, especially in meetings. If you run your own small or large business, delegation is not permission to be in the dark about the inner workings or processes of your business. Even if you choose to hire someone to run your company, you should still have a knowledge of what they do and what they know. They may need to provide you with updates and reports on certain aspects of the business because you have successfully and completely delegated, but when it is all said and done, the responsibility and liability of your company lies with you. Would you simply trust everything that your accountant told you about the money that was coming in and going out of your business or would you sit down with them on a biweekly, monthly or quarterly basis to figure out where these dollars are being spent? While operations is not necessarily the most exciting or sexy part of any business, it is crucial and essential for you, as a business owner, to have a firm grasp of the big picture and enough of the details to make effective decisions. Delegate, but don't be in the dark.

"FORGETTING" YOUR WAY THROUGH LIFE

I can guarantee I am not the only one who has ever walked into a room and, moments later, thought, "Now why did I come in here?" How in the world then, do we think we can remember all of the things we need to get done? We write grocery lists because there is just no way we can remember all of it.

No matter how smart we are, how high our IQ, or our scholastic accomplishments, human memory is a flawed system. While our brains are wonderfully made, they have their limits. We remember what we truly want to remember, that which matters to us, marks us, shapes us or otherwise is significant to us, and the rest floats along a gray matter highway on cruise control until we need it. It may pop up again because something reminds us of it, but who wants to live so unintentionally?

I have a friend who recently forgot a very important event, one which literally only occurs once in someone's lifetime. She forgot to attend a memorial service for a college friend. If you miss a birthday party, the chances are you will be able to attend next year's. However, weddings, baby showers, and funerals are probably things you don't want to miss. It stung, especially since I had planned the entire event, but I was mostly disappointed for her sake, since this was also a dear friend of hers.

A former colleague of mine would often forget his way through his day. It was a wonder that he ever made it to our numerous weekly meetings. I would sometimes be in his office when he took phone calls. At the end of the call, he would say, "Yes, I will take care of that and get back to you." However, upon hanging up, there was not a single 'note to self' about what it was he had just promised. He received complaint after complaint as he often over-promised and under-delivered.

While forgetting hurts those in our lives, it also hurts us. Once the event is over, it's over, and you don't get a do-over.

These two occurrences made me think of my mom's forever-repeated adage, *"The faintest ink is more powerful than the strongest memory,"* which originated as a Chinese Proverb. Let's face it, we are ALL forgetful, and to be totally honest, even though I was planning my friend's memorial, I may have even forgotten if it wasn't on my calendar. The reason why I am so effective in getting so much done, and remembering all that I have to do has absolutely nothing to do with my memory, and while I have a pretty good one, there is no way I can hold all the dates, times, and appointments in my head.

This is why the day planner and organization industry, even amidst the digital era continues to be an enterprise worth over half a billion dollars, driving the point that people spend a lot of money to not forget. If you write it in your day planner, be sure to look at it throughout your day or week. Even better, if you are prone to forgetting, you can use the trusty reminder systems built into digital calendars that will alert you at any set interval you choose. For example you can set an alarm two hours before you're supposed to be somewhere to remind yourself that you actually have an appointment. There is no shame in setting reminders for yourself. We all have a lot going on in our lives, and things that pull us in a variety of directions. In the era of buzzers, bells, dings and whistles, we can no longer use "I forgot" as an excuse. If you want to be successful, keep your commitments, be known as someone who is trustworthy and reliable, and write it down!

THE MYTH OF MULTITASKING

Have you ever watched a movie and talked on the phone at the same time? What usually happens is one of two things. Either you are completely into your movie and whoever is on the other line feels totally ignored, or you are fully engaged in the conversation, and once you are finished, you have to start the movie over because you missed everything. The same is true for what we like to call multitasking. I am not talking about putting the laundry in the wash and then starting dinner; that's just efficient. Multitasking refers to performing two or more tasks simultaneously, switching back and forth from one thing to another, or performing a number of tasks in rapid succession.

Research has shown that while multitasking seems like a great way to accomplish multiple tasks at once, it has been revealed that our brains are not nearly as good at handling this as we like to think. Some researchers suggest that multitasking can actually reduce productivity by as much as 40%.

The truth of it is, when we think we are multitasking, what we are actually doing is quickly shifting our focus from one task to the next. This switching back and forth makes it difficult to tune out distractions and can cause mental blocks that can slow you down.

Take a moment to think about all of the things you are doing right now. Obviously, you are reading this book, but odds are you are in the middle of doing several things. Maybe you're listening to music, texting a friend, checking your email or playing a game on your phone.

Multitaskers have more trouble tuning out distractions than people who focus on one task at a time. Also, doing so many different things at once can impair your cognitive abilities.

Studies measuring the time impact of multitasking showed that when participants were asked to switch tasks, they were slower than when they repeated the same task, and they lost even more time as the tasks became increasingly complex.

For some people, the ability to focus on one thing at a time is no problem at all. However, for me, this has proven to be a major challenge over the course of my life, in both my work and personal life.

When in the working world I would often have several tabs open on my computer. I'd work on a project, then moments later check an email, then make a phone call, then pop into my calendar, then back to the project, and it was causing me to feel frenzied and scatterbrained throughout my work day.

Initially, I thought it was my need to keep things fresh and avoid boredom, but in reality, I had not trained my brain to be disciplined and focused. I decided I would instead spend a solid hour or two concentrating on a singular task. I was most certainly tempted to go back to my old ways, and it took the practice of closing all other tabs and forcing myself to engage solely on the task at hand.

After staying the course and creating a habit, it not only changed the way I viewed my work day, but it also allowed me to feel much less frantic and much more peaceful and calm throughout the day. To top it off, once I had successfully focused on one project and completed it, I had a better sense of accomplishment at the end of my day, and learned that having one finished project is so much more gratifying than many unfinished ones.

THE FUNDAMENTALS OF FOLLOW THROUGH

Have you ever heard the term, "Fortune is in the follow up?" I am not sure where this quote derives, I just remember hearing it once at a seminar, and it has never left me. The speaker used it in reference to networking, saying that you can make connections and collect a bunch of business cards, but if you never follow up, you will have essentially missed potentially beneficial opportunities. I could not even begin to count the number of times someone said, "Hey, we should get together some time." I would wholeheartedly agree, and then I would never hear back. In fact, if I weren't the one reaching back out to make the appointment, it most likely would not have happened. This is not to toot my own horn. I'm simply saying that we often say things, with great intentions or make ambitious plans, but rarely take the time to follow through, thus it fizzles out before it was ever given a chance to be born.

The same can be said for our dreams, goals, and desired accomplishments. The difference between a sheer dreamer and the one who achieves is follow-up and follow-through. If you are not the one pushing the meter forward, no one else will. Trust me, this takes a great deal of discipline. It is much easier to be the "ideas guy." Follow-up and follow through is far from exciting or alluring. It fits right in line with the slow, and often painful drudgery of the daily, and often mundane and tedious tasks it takes to push a goal forward. However, if you want to accomplish anything, and I do mean anything, if you don't follow through, you will never reach the finish line. One way for me to remember to follow up with someone about a conversation or appointment is to write it down in my calendar, showing up something like this, "Follow up with so and so regarding x, y and z." If I don't remind myself, I too will forget.

PRESSED FOR TIME

Would you buy a diet pill from someone who has been skinny all of their life or someone who has struggled with their weight and, because of this pill, has seen a marked difference in their body as a result? We like stories of real people who have overcome real adversity, rather than people who seem to have it all together, because imperfect people relate to imperfect people.

Now is my turn to reveal my imperfection, the chink in my armor. Wait for it...I am not always on time! Gasp! Before you throw the book across the room and ask for a refund, please hear me out.

Being on time is where my relationship with time has suffered the most. With the exception of job interviews and auditions, where I know being late has dire consequences, I can easily be ten minutes late to any given appointment, work meeting, or social encounter. Raise your hand if you can relate. In this section, I am going to break down the areas that cause me to struggle with being on time, and the things that I do to keep myself accountable.

The Five Reasons I Find Myself Running Late

Mindset

Our thinking has so much to do with how we function in life; it informs most, if not all of our decisions, whether subconscious or conscious. We've heard the saying, if you are on time, you are late. For me, if I am on time, I am on time, and that is an accomplishment all by itself, especially since it generally takes so much of my energy and effort to do so. When it came to showing up to appointments with friends and family, I built in a self-appointed grace period of five to fifteen minutes, and would also extend this same courtesy to the people in my life. However, I quickly learned who was okay with this and who was not. For those who were not, I started to earn a reputation for untimeliness, and it was those same people who would make known their surprise when I was on time.

It was through these experiences that I learned that timeliness is so much more than the numbers on a clock, but rather a matter of respecting people and their time. Hence, when I was habitually late some people interpreted it as me not respecting their time.

Working Up to the Last Minute & Not Building in Enough Time for Transitions

I often work on projects back-to-back. I don't generally build in break times, but naturally know when my body and mind is done with a task. As someone who loves accomplishing things, I can easily get swept away into the zone of an endeavor, and by the time I look up, I realize that I now have to transition to my next appointment.

The practice of building in transitions takes more than a notion. It takes planning, foresight and effort. Let's say you have a meeting that ends at 1:00 p.m., and you have something scheduled across town, at 1:30 p.m. Provided that appointment is a mere ten minutes away we may find ourselves in a serious frenzy trying to get there, and Heaven forbid the meeting runs over. Just getting out of the meeting alone can take a few minutes, gathering your belongings, and saying your goodbyes. Let's not forget about the time it takes to get to your vehicle, plug in the address, and head on your way. You not only have to account for how much time it may take to get there, but you will need to build in time for potential road hazards, traffic, weather or otherwise unforeseen issues.

Transition time is something very important and not to be ignored. It is the "to" in your point A "to" point B. Transition times can include taking care of your physical needs - using the restroom, grabbing a bite to eat, or your mental needs - taking a moment to rest your mind, or simply the time in transit to your next event. If you don't properly build in these seemingly mundane, but crucial moments, you will often find yourself running late. For someone like me, a do-er who has been known to try and squeeze as much into my day as possible, I need to be very deliberate to build in these very important transition times.

My Disdain for Wasting Time

One of the reasons why I find myself running late is because I loathe wasting time. For example, before navigation, when we actually had to find our way to places I could not stand to find out I took the long route somewhere. In meetings back when I worked in the nine-to-five sector, and people would blab on and on, repeating the same concepts over and over, and over and over (ok, that was for effect), I would cringe and look at my watch, thinking, this is such a waste of time. For some reason, in my mind, the thought of showing up somewhere 10 to 15 minutes early made me think about how much I could be doing with that time versus just sitting and waiting for my appointment. Even as I say it out loud, I realize I could probably take my own advice from sections like "Killing Time," "Doing While Doing," or "Boredom Is Not an Option." Until writing this book, though, it simply felt like wasted time to me. So next time I show up somewhere early, I'll bring a book and chip away at a chapter or two, or watch a video on something I'd like to learn, so that that precious time is not wasted.

Not Liking to Be Put in a Box

While I am certainly someone who tends to obey the laws of the land, there is a part of me that is slightly rebellious. I don't like being put in a box and I struggle when things are too rigid, legalistic, and don't allow for fluidity and creativity. For this reason, I have found that it is difficult to be confined by time, and while I am acutely aware of the reality of time, it is not always my friend. Rushing around to fit myself within the limitations of time causes me to feel confined and restricted.

My need to Live on the Edge

There was a time when my car was in the shop for an extended period, and for that reason, I needed to borrow a friend's car to run some errands. Knowing my tendency for pushing the envelope of time, I told her I'd come 30 minutes before her appointment time so I could drop her off and then take the car. She said, "Girl, the appointment is like 5 minutes up the street." When the day came, I still tried my best to be 30 minutes early, but you guessed it, I was running a bit behind on my proposed schedule. I let her know my ETA and headed on my merry way, with her words still ringing in my head. I picked her up with exactly five minutes to get to her appointment (which she was on time to).

However, in the car ride over, I could tell she was upset. She expressed to me that she didn't want to get to her appointment right on time. I'll admit, I was baffled. Didn't she tell me not to rush and that her appointment was only five minutes up the street? I was sitting there thinking, "How can you be mad if you are going to be on time?" However, she wanted a bigger cushion, thus not wanting to show up right on time. For me, being on time is the victory, but I had to realize that some people don't like to push it so closely. This is when I had the epiphany for the fifth and final reason why I tend to run late. I actually really like the thrill and the sense of living on the edge, and while this stresses some people out, it helps me to feel invigorated and alive. Much like my love of roller coasters and driving fast cars, I get a similar thrill when pushing the time envelope, but I realize now that most people don't like to live like this, and therefore I need to be mindful of this.

METHODS FOR STAYING ON TIME

I was recently in a job where I had to punch a clock. Not only did I have to drive 25 minutes to work, but I had to park, then walk to the job. It was such a struggle for me, and most days I was anywhere between two to six minutes late, probably for the majority of the year-and-a-half that I worked there. It wasn't until I had a conversation with one of my coworkers who was close to both of the managers that I realized the gravity of this. She told me that I would actually be the perfect employee if it weren't for my tardiness, and then said this was the one thing my bosses were watching most. After that conversation, I had a talk with God about this. He gently said to me, "You rush to work, and you're still late, why not rush and be on time?" That was my ah-ha moment, and from that point on I can happily say I have grown so much in this area.

If you are at all like me, and can identify with any of the above-mentioned challenges with relation to timeliness, here are a few methods to aid you on your quest.

Give Yourself More Time Than You Actually Need

If you think you need thirty minutes to get to your destination, build in a cushion of an extra 15 to 20 minutes. This will help to ensure you are on time, and it will also give you a peace of mind knowing you will not be running up to the last minute. This cushion can allow for unforeseen issues, like traffic, allow you to park and walk, sweat-free to your next destination.

Work Backwards

When I know I need to travel to an appointment, especially one that is in the first part of my day I also have to factor in how much time it will take to get ready. Working backwards (something we will discuss more later) might look something like this. Let's say I have an appointment at 10:00 a.m., and it is a half-hour from my home. You should probably give yourself a 20 minute cushion, so you need to leave your house by 9:10 a.m. It takes you 1.5 hours to get ready, which means you should be awake by 7:30 a.m. (with a small 10 minute cushion for anything unforeseen). If you need eight hours of sleep then you'll want to be in bed by 11:00 p.m. so you can be asleep by 11:30 p.m. In my city, I often need to double the amount of time I give myself because we have severe traffic issues. You will be surprised at how many people run late because they do not do this type of pre-planning.

Set Alarms

At a previous job I would set alarms for when I needed to show up to my next Zoom meeting, because again, I could easily get caught up in a project and miss my call time. I would set an alarm 10 minutes before, then five minutes before, and sometimes even two minutes before the actual meeting. This also helps for when I have important phone calls to make.

Sometimes I even set alarms for when I need to start getting ready for bed. As a night owl, the discipline is more about going to bed on time rather than being up on time. If I go to bed at a reasonable hour, getting up is easy breezy.

BENEFITS OF BEING ON TIME

- Feeling peace and calm versus feeling rushed and frazzled upon arrival
- Plenty of time to find parking
- Time to get acquainted with your surroundings when you arrive
- People often trust you more when you are on time versus having the reputation as someone who is always late
- When you arrive early to events such as church or seminars you can get a better seat
- Being on time, or even early, allows you to get to know the people around you at your event or meeting
- The satisfaction of respecting someone's time

JENNIFER F. ARTHUR'S - THE 24 HOUR CURRENCY
REVIEW REQUEST PAGE

Unlock the power of generosity and make a difference with your review!

"You can't do anything about the length of your life, but you can do something about its depth."

— UNKNOWN

We all know time is precious. We save it, spend it, waste it, and wish we had more of it. But what if you could help someone else change their relationship with time—just by sharing your thoughts?

That's where you come in...

If *The 24 Hour Currency* meant something to you—if it opened your eyes, made you think, helped you feel more in control of your time—I have one simple request:

Would you leave a review?

Here's the thing: Most people don't buy a book unless it has reviews. They want to know it's worth their time (because, as we know, time is a big deal). Your review might be the one that helps someone decide *this* is the book that could help them live differently.

It only takes a minute. Costs nothing. But it could make a huge impact.

Your review could help...

- One more small business owner breathe easier.
- One more dreamer chase that "someday" goal.
- One more overwhelmed parent find peace.
- One more person stop saying "I'll do it later" and start saying "Why not now?"
- One more life turn from busy to purposeful.

If you're the kind of person who believes in lifting others up, in sharing what works, in helping someone else take back their time—then you're my kind of person, ***and I thank you in advance for taking your time, energy and heart to post a review on whichever platform you purchased your copy!***

With deep gratitude,

Jennifer F. Arthur

11
TIME MANAGEMENT TACTICS

WORKING BACKWARDS

It was during college that I learned the art and science of working backwards, and I genuinely cannot emphasize how this skill has saved me so many headaches and heartaches throughout the course of my life. In addition to ensuring you show up to places on time, this tactic can be applied to many other areas of your life - event planning, DIY projects, completing timely school assignments, and more.

When the first week of school rolled around, I would take all of my syllabi and mark the deadlines for papers, projects, and exams in my calendar. From there, I would estimate how much time I needed to complete each paper or assignment. If it were a paper that was due on October 30th, for example, I figured I needed at least three weeks to comfortably and effectively complete it. At that point, I'd determine how much time was necessary for research, how much time I would need to write, and how much time I needed to allot for rewrites and editing. By the time the due dates rolled around, I was cool, calm, and collected while confidently handing in my assignments to my professors. I strongly believe that using the method of working backwards was the largest contributor to my high GPA. Once you have mastered the skill of working backwards you will truly thank yourself.

KEEPING A TIME LOG

Many people keep logs for various reasons. Some people log their workouts, food and water intake, or budgets. Why not keep a daily time log? You can put it in an Excel sheet, a paper journal, or in the notes on your phone. Whatever works for you. I have provided a sample ***Daily Time Log*** (See Appendix).

Such a document can help you more efficiently steward your time and will give you a glimpse into exactly how you are spending it, with the hopes that you can recover some of it by mending broken habits.

Perhaps you notice on your log that you are using a lot of time on social media during your prime time hours, and want to shift that activity to your downtime. Maybe you realize that there are chunks of time in your day that you cannot account for at all.

I suggest you log your time for at least two weeks so you can track your trends. You will note that on the log, there is a space for the activity, a start time, and an end time. Be sure to put in both times so that you can see the exact amount of time you spent on each activity you log.

Much like when you log your food, you are much less likely to eat that whole bag of Oreos. The exercise of logging your time will help you to pay closer attention to how you use your time, with the goal of creating more awareness, accountability and ultimately improvements.

THE POWER OF A WORK/CREATIVE SPRINT

The practice of HIIT (High Intensity Interval Training) has long been a trend in the fitness world. Essentially, it is a method in which you go full out for a short period of time, followed by a rest phase. For instance, running on the treadmill for a two-minute sprint, followed by walking for three minutes. You can do this, in cycles, between 15 and 40 minutes. This is an incredible method for increasing your metabolism and seeing major weight loss results.

This same type of process can apply when working on projects. It can look something like this: you sprint for one hour on your writing, budget, planning, painting, editing photos or other such work-related tasks. Then give yourself a period of rest for 15 to 20 minutes. You can use this time to completely veg out or use it to do smaller, less intense tasks, like making a phone call, grabbing a snack, checking email, chatting with a coworker, or using the restroom. Much as the rest period in HIIT gives our bodies the recovery time it needs in order to go all out again, the same applies to the break in our creative or work sprint. Here's to that metaphorical six pack!

CONSULT YOUR CALENDAR BEFORE COMMITTING

I have most certainly made the mistake early in my life, both professionally and personally, where I made a commitment to someone only to have to go back to them and tell them that I double booked. If you have ever done this, you know how embarrassing it feels. Other than the feeling of embarrassment it appears disorganized, and we all know I feel about that!

After a few of these embarrassing blunders, I made it a point to never make a commitment without first checking my calendar. Even if I am ninety-nine percent certain that I am available, I still check and get back to the person when I am absolutely sure that there is an undivided space on my calendar for them.

PERSONAL TIME MANAGEMENT BREAKTHROUGHS

I have been known to squeeze a lot of projects into a week. As of late, I have been feeling like I am stretched too thin and pulled in too many different directions. So, I have changed my system of how I organize my week. Instead of trying to make progress on two or three large projects every day, I have started staggering them onto different days of the week, and depending on the project, sometimes even onto different weeks within the month.

For example, instead of working on my book, screenplay, and a design client every day of the week, I would work on the design client Monday and Wednesday, the book on Tuesday and Thursday, and the screenplay on Saturday. I feel like this strategy has given me a better grasp and more flow and traction on my projects. I also used to arbitrarily scatter smaller tasks or errands throughout my week, but I found that this interrupted my flow and made it harder to focus on larger, more important tasks. Instead, I decided to use one day per week, typically Fridays, as a catch-all day for errands, non-essential phone calls, and other non-urgent tasks.

This small tweak to my system has really changed my effectiveness, given me a better grasp on my time, and a greater sense of accomplishment.

Keep in mind that your systems can change as well. There is nothing set in stone with respect to how you manage yourself within your time. If one system is not working, scrap it and find another.

12
SHRINKING & GROWING TIME

"Lost wealth may be replaced by industry, lost knowledge by study, lost health by temperance or medicine, but lost time is gone forever."

— SAMUEL SMILES

In the last couple of chapters, we discussed ways you can save, spend, cherish, and conserve your time. In this section, we will consider ways in which you can mitigate time wasters and how you can further stretch, save, maximize, and use your time purposefully and effectively.

"TIK TOK"

It should be called 'tick tock', like that of a clock, as the minutes and hours silently melt away, lost in a sea of other people's content. Any time management or success guru will say the same thing: social media is a terrible time suck. To be clear, I do have Facebook and

Instagram, and will do an occasional scroll during my downtime in an effort to veg out. Let me also say that there are positive uses to social media. For example, I have learned many helpful skills on YouTube, and while I do not personally have a TikTok account, I know many people also use that as a means of learning. There are many friends from my past who have tracked me down after years of hiatus, and I can watch the children of my friends grow up on sites like Facebook. However, the arguments against social media by those who have gone before me are strongly advocating for the fact that if you are not careful you will simply be throwing your time into a fire pit.

Before you go down the rabbit hole of cyber bliss, try instituting the *daily time log* method in an effort to keep yourself accountable. Track the time you start and when you stop, and do this for an entire week, and see how much time you spent on it. You can also set a timer for a predetermined amount of time and keep yourself accountable by logging off the site once you hear the alarm. I'd even go so far as to dare you to fast from social media for a week, and see what happens with your effectiveness. Obviously, if you are a social media influencer or a marketing professional, and this is your source of income, I am not talking to you. However, for the rest of us, this is likely not the case.

In addition to sucking up valuable time and keeping us from our goals, social media has often been used as a time filler. I see people scrolling endlessly at the gym and in the sauna, walking. It is literally like a drug, and what most drugs do is keep us from our true selves. What is wrong with simply having time of silence in our minds to be able to think, reflect, meditate or just old-fashioned people watch. The more we escape through social media, the less our brains get a chance to exercise on thinking through complex issues, daydreaming or even coming up with the next big idea.

Some of my most creative, ah-ha moments have come from times of quiet reflection, on a walk (without headphones), in the car, in the shower, sitting along the coast. These times of quiet have created a number of amazing things - movie ideas, songs, solutions to relationship issues, and even this book. If I were always scrolling, I would literally miss those treasured moments. Give it a try. Think about what you could come up with if you decided to stop clogging yourself with other people's content.

TIME BANDITS

Below is a (non-exhaustive) list of pesky habits that can rob our time:

1. **Television** - With streaming services at an all-time high, we have more options for entertainment than at any other time in our history. Trust me, I have my share of favorite shows, and especially as I have recently taken up screenwriting, it is essential to keep up with the TV Jones', although, even in that, I set boundaries for myself. I allow myself up to two hours of indulging, at any one setting. I generally only turn on the television at the end of the day (during my down-time), once I have completed all my tasks for the day.
2. **Social media** - As previously discussed, social media can easily become a rabbit hole of wasted time - whether videos of cute little kittens, political discourse, or simply looking at photos of your friend's last adventure, you can look up and realize you have spent a couple of hours of your life, scrolling.
3. **Daydreaming** - We all do this, but doing it for extended amounts of time can be a real detriment to your time.
4. **Being overwhelmed** - If we let it, overwhelm can paralyze us. If this is something you struggle with, re-read the section entitled "One Day at a Time" at the beginning of chapter 10 - Time Management 101).

5. **Not planning** - Poor planning can be a major headache, and waste so much valuable time putting out fires, having to retrace your steps, and otherwise running around in a frenzy in order to successfully pull off your event, trip or other endeavors.
6. **Talking on the phone for extended periods of time** - I am not referring to not spending time catching up with a friend or family member, but rather being on the phone and not talking about anything substantial (i.e. what my aunts coined as "Reality Phone" - being on the phone while the other person goes about their daily life, while you virtually tag along). Trust me, we've all done it!
7. **Not making decisions in a timely fashion** - This could lead to the loss of important opportunities, which costs time.
8. **Incessantly venting or complaining** - Especially if you are not looking for the solution.
9. **Being disorganized** - It takes time to look for things you cannot find. Devise a system of organization for your life that works best for you. *One note:* I always put my keys in the same place when I arrive home. I believe this has contributed to the fact that I can only think of maybe one time in my life that I have lost my keys.
10. **The paralysis of analysis** - As we have seen in the section on the "Get 'er Done Continuum ," being paralyzed by overanalyzing every decision can cost you hours, weeks, days, and if you are not careful, years of your life.
11. **Aiming for perfection** - We know no one is perfect, and if you know it, other people know it. So why do we push so hard to be perfect? People relate much more to flawed humans than to those who appear to be "perfect." Perfectionism is a symptom of a greater insecurity. Self-aware, imperfect people give grace to other imperfect

people. If we let go of some of the control that comes with perfectionism, that will save us valuable time.

12. **Dilly dallying** - Directionless and pointless actions. This can also be a symptom of a lack of motivation or being scattered in your mind.
13. **Worrying** - You cannot add a single hour to your life - in fact, worrying is one of the quickest ways to lose precious time. Obsessing about "what if" cannot change the situation. To be clear, worry is different from strategizing, planning or praying for a solution, which is quite healthy and effective. In addition, worry and anxiety only add to your stress levels, which increases cortisol. Too much cortisol can lead to a variety of other ailments, which can lead to more worry. In order to be mentally and physically healthy, find ways to decrease worry.
14. **People pleasing** - Of course, we cannot go through life not considering how our actions affect other people. However, there is a careful line we must tow. On the one end of the spectrum we can be people pleasers, caring incessantly about every thought that someone has about us, and on the other, we can air air-toward complete rebellion, bulldozing our way through life. We must find a balance. The problem with caring too much about what others think of us is that we become paralyzed and confused when it comes to making those very important life decisions because we care about what everyone else thinks, and this can not only steal our time, but our joy as well.
15. **Poor communication** - Faulty communication, miscommunication and a lack of communication can cost a great deal of time.
16. **Trying to be right/proving people wrong** - We live in an information age. I have been a part of and been witness to conversations where one person tells the other, "Look it up", referring to researching whatever is the topic of debate.

In a relationship, a good one, that is, arguing and bickering about trivial matters only wastes the time you could otherwise be spending enjoying one another's company. Not to mention the time it takes to research a topic just so that you can prove to that person that you were right. More importantly, nobody likes a know-it-all.

17. **Holding grudges, unresolved anger and unforgiveness** - There is not a person on the planet who has not endured some type of injury from another human being. After the original injury, it will take some time to heal, and at some point, you will be faced with the decision of whether or not to forgive that person. Bitterness, unresolved anger, and unforgiveness only hurt the person who is harboring them. There are many studies and many books about the mind, body, and spirit connection. It is impossible to hold onto anger and be a fully fulfilled individual. Spending too much time in the pain, not allowing yourself to heal, or keeping the anger inside can eventually manifest in your body, leading to physical disease, which can ultimately take years off your life.
18. **Pursuing a profession for which you're not passionate** - How many people live their lives doing work they hate? Life is too short to not do what you have been designed for - that thing which you excel at, and brings you inexplicable joy. Don't let your days pass by doing something that brings you no joy, for example, going to medical school when all you want to do is act.
19. **Haste (makes waste)** - This saying basically says it all. When you do things in a hurry, it can lead to mishaps, which ultimately take time to correct.
20. **Procrastination** - Each day that passes is a day that can bring you closer to your goals. Don't wait for the perfect time, because that will never come.

MAXIMIZING YOUR TIME (DOING WHILE DOING)

Whether you spend a lot of time scheduling or you are more inclined to live by the seat of your pants, as humans, we share some common activities: eating, working, sleeping, and spending time with others. In addition, we all have the time that lies in between those activities. It is during these lag times that we can fill with small chores and tasks that are on our to-do list or even things you can never seem to find the time for. I once had a job, working background on TV and film sets. After two times on set with absolutely nothing to do in between shots, I wised up and started taking my computer to set. As a writer, this was incredible! I was being paid to work on my own stuff. What other job allows for that? In fact, I worked on this book on multiple sets. While this may not relate to you, the moral is that we all have lulls in time that we can utilize for productivity. I'm not suggesting you never let your mind rest, but there are times we are stuck in a time suck, like standing in line, or on a long car ride. Here are some ways we can take advantage of these times.

While you're talking on the phone - With bluetooth and headsets, it is easier than ever to use your free hands to do other mindless tasks during phone calls, such as: washing dishes, folding laundry, packing/unpacking from a trip, cooking, organizing files, clipping your nails, and on and on and on.

While you're in the bathroom - Let's be real, everybody poops, there's even a children's story about it. If you take an extended amount of time in the loo, why not use it to your advantage? Planning, reading, watching your favorite show, sending emails, all thanks to modern technology are possible while in the can. If you are going to be there for more than 10 minutes, you can really put a dent in your to (doo-doo) list.

While you eat (alone) - Generally speaking, it is best to mindfully enjoy your food, to avoid overeating, or eating too quickly. However, if you do choose to use this opportunity to knock out some of your to-do list, activities like reading an article, meal planning, creating your grocery lists, or looking over your calendar could be a good use of this time.

While you watch TV - You can use this time to sort or fold laundry, fill your weekly vitamin box, give yourself a manicure/pedicure, or stretch. All activities that take minimal mental capacity, so as not to distract you from enjoying your favorite show.

While you're in the car - Some of us live in big cities, and with that comes a lot of commute time, and traffic! Los Angeles alone has over 10 million people, and it seems like all of them are driving on the 405 Freeway between 5:00 - 8:00 p.m. Avoid the frustration that comes with heavy traffic, and turn on your favorite tunes, pop on a podcast or audiobook or call your grandma (because you know you feel guilty you don't call her enough). No one will fault you for calling them while you're on the road; they'll just be happy to hear from you (be sure you are using a hands-free device like Bluetooth or headsets to avoid costly distractions). If one of those things isn't your cup of tea, you can try using that time to reflect on your workday. Maybe you had a falling out with a loved one in the morning. Use the time to rethink how you could have done things differently. Perhaps you feel like you are not performing the way you want to at work or you're contemplating finding a new job. Use the time to come up with a plan. This can also be a good time for connecting with your higher power, dreaming about your future, your kids' or family's future, or vacations you want to take. Maybe you're a writer or songwriter, and you are struck with an idea, use the microphone function on your phone to create a couple of chapters in your next book or a couple bars of your next song. I have been known to do this.

While waiting in line - This is a good time to check email or social feeds, read an article on your phone or grab a magazine off the rack. Otherwise, it's a good time to connect with those around you and simply be human.

When someone else is driving, carpooling, or taking public transportation, you can work on projects, check emails, catch up on reading, writing, listen to an audio book or podcast, or simply daydream.

While cooking - This is a great time to listen to audiobooks, watch "how to" videos, or talk on the phone.

KILLING TIME

Similar to doing while doing, we often have moments in between appointments that can feel like wasted time. You can most certainly use this time to refresh, reflect, and recharge before your next meeting. However, if you are more like me, you may feel the need to fill in this gap. It may not necessarily be enough time to do a full project or hold an actual appointment, but enough time to do *something.* The time in between can be used to do a variety of productive tasks.

Some time killing ideas:

1. Sew that button or stitch that seam you keep saying you'll get around to. Wait, do people still sew? Some of us do ;)
2. Look through magazines for images for your yearly vision board
3. Clean out those empty glass spice bottles that you have been wanting to reuse
4. Make a phone call to someone you don't call nearly enough
5. Write a thank you note to that neighbor who helped you out or to a friend whom you simply want to appreciate
6. Research something you have been thinking about, but never make the time to explore
7. Organize:
    - Photos
    - Spice rack
    - Junk drawer
    - Sock drawer

- Underwear drawer
- Food container drawer
- Craft space
- Tool box
- Files
- Desk

8. Make a list of gifts you want to buy people
9. Do some planning in your calendar for your next day/week/month
10. Grooming: file your nails, pluck your eyebrows, groom your beard
11. Iron some clothes you never get around to ironing
12. Separate laundry
13. Catch up on reading (books, articles, audio books)
14. Listen to your favorite podcast, TED Talk, etc.

BOREDOM IS NOT AN OPTION

Since childhood I've always been pretty good at entertaining myself, but on the rare occasion I would ever utter the words "I'm bored," my mother would say, "Only boring people are bored." It was a harsh statement, but it only took a couple of times before I stopped with that complaint. Even then I realized she was right, and since that time, I have been a person who refuses to be bored.

My first job was at a retail clothing store. My boss' motto was, "If you have nothing to do, you can always find something to do." She was right, there was always a shirt to fold or a dust bunny to sweep.

In both these instances, what my mother and my boss were saying was to think outside of the norm, and *create* something to do with your time.

Here is a list of ways to stave off boredom:

1. Personal growth - listen to podcasts, read self-development books - like this one :)
2. Home improvement projects - even if you live in an apartment, there are things you can do to make your space more enjoyable.
3. Exercise
4. Watch a TV show
5. Go for a walk - (This is obviously a form of exercise, which is mentioned above; however, unlike some other types of exercise, walking has been known to stimulate our imagination and innovation)
6. Watch the sunset
7. Clean up your emails or computer files
8. Cook/bake
9. Learn a new skill (YouTube "University")
10. Clean your home
11. Puzzles (crossword and otherwise)
12. Journal
13. Meditate
14. Plan your week
15. Meal prep
16. Sing or play an instrument
17. Brainstorm business ideas or other endeavors
18. Plan and research a place in which you hope to take a trip

OTHER RANDOM WAYS TO SAVE & MAXIMIZE YOUR TIME

- ***Make your lunch/breakfast the night before*** - If you're like me you need every second of time in the morning, so I always make my lunch at night, and have my lunch bag in the fridge. This often includes a ready-made breakfast, something easy to eat on the go, like: fruit and nuts, a boiled egg, yogurt, or a breakfast bar. In the morning, it's all in one place, ready for me to simply grab and go.
- ***Clean as you go (especially when you cook)*** - This was something engrained in me by my mother. While I don't generally wash the dishes during the time of cooking, I will stack the dishwasher as I finish with a dish or utensil, and wipe counters. In addition, I put away all the ingredients and spices as I finish with them. I have found that this helps me to better enjoy the meal that I just prepared, for two reasons: 1) When I look into the kitchen, as I am eating the delicious meal I labored over, I'm not reminded by the tornado-like mess that there is yet more work to be done. 2) Once I finish cooking and eating a delicious meal, the last thing I want to do is spend more time on my feet, cleaning the kitchen. Cleaning as you go literally only adds seconds in the moment, whereas cleaning everything after could easily take up to an hour.
- ***Prepare your outfits the night before*** - Much like preparing your lunch/breakfast the night before, this will save time rifling through your closet in the morning, running the risk of indecisiveness, and potential wardrobe changes. Again, if you are like me, you need all that precious morning time. Preparing clothes can include simply thinking through what you will wear, or actually pulling the outfits and setting them aside, and if need be, ironing them.

- ***Clean your dashboard while in the drive-through car wash*** - Keep your Armor All or other cleaning aids nearby so that you can have a clean dash by the time you make it out of the car wash.
- ***Unbunch your socks as you take them off*** - This also only takes seconds, and saves you from having to unbunch them all on laundry day, which can be quite time-consuming.
- ***Iron multiple pieces of clothing at a time*** - If you're already ironing a shirt or a pair of pants, why not do multiple pieces in one sitting? This way, you don't have to go through the hassle of pulling out the ironing board every time you need to get ready.

13
PLANNING (ORGANIZING) 101

"If you fail to plan, plan to fail."

— BENJAMIN FRANKLIN

There is so much to say on this topic, and quite frankly, I could write a whole book about it. Before we dive into the world of planning, let's first look at some industries and professionals who, by not planning, would utterly fail. A captain of a ship plans out their course; otherwise, they would be aimlessly traveling through open waters, running the risk of being lost at sea. A football coach plans their team's plays before the game starts, and even goes so far as to study their opponents' strengths and weaknesses. Companies plan, often an entire year in advance, for their sales, marketing, and finance departments, and the list goes on.

Authors Brian P. Moran and Michael Lennington, of *The 12 Week Year,* state that we are 60-80 times more likely to execute a plan that is on paper than one that is simply in our heads because writing it down eliminates ambiguity.

While planning may entail a bit of skill and a smidge of artistry, it is primarily a decision. The wonderful thing about planning is that it is not brain surgery, and virtually anyone can do it. It does, however, take some discipline and intentionality. Proper planning could be the difference between securing a client or not, catching your flight on time or not, and successfully meeting a project deadline or not. Planning helps us not to have to live with our hair on fire or in constant emergency mode. It creates peace and gives our lives structure.

A coworker once asked, on the day of a major event that I had been planning for over a month, "How are you so calm?" I told him that the work had already been taken care of in all of the planning. Now it was just plug and chug. I went on to tell him, cool as a cucumber, that if anything went wrong that day, it was not for lack of planning.

Overall, organization is a trifecta of prioritizing, time management, and effective planning. In the following section, we will further discuss planning and how we personally show up in this space. In addition, I will share some planning tools that I use on a consistent basis for mapping out my years, months, weeks, and days.

THE PLANNER SPECTRUM

It is clear by now that I often see the world in the form of continuums. In my opinion, there is no hard or fast rule for anything. As humans, we are varied, diverse, and complex beings. Moving forward, we will assess various planning personality types (See graph below).

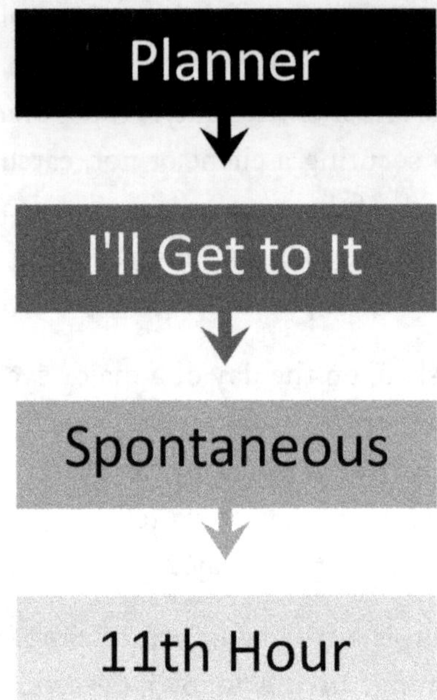

The "Planner"

We all have those friends, the ones who if we went on vacation with they'd have mapped out every minute of every day. You'd hope to sip on a Mai Tai while soaking up the sun, and maybe reading that book you lugged along with you, but there they are watching you, as you breathe softly under your sun hat. You feel their glare and can see it in their eyes. They're bored, and their agenda is burning a hole in their beach bag. While these people may cause anxiety for some of the people around them, this is their very sense of peace. The peace that only order and knowing what's next can bring. On the downside, these Type A people are often wound pretty tightly, and find it hard to relax and go with the flow. Their world is turned upside down with the slightest change of events in the "plan." True confession, in many ways, I am this person, especially when I am wearing my business hat. In graduate school, I was this person in most of my groups, wanting to map out each of our steps and processes for the completion of our group project. It wasn't until then that I learned this type of "over planning" made my Type B classmates anxious. Since then, I have had to learn that when it comes to my plans, I need to use my inside voice, meaning I need to keep my plans to myself. It doesn't mean I don't have a plan or even all the steps of my process and desired outcome mapped out. I have simply had to discern with whom I can share these thoughts, and with whom I cannot, in order to keep everyone's, including my inner planner, at peace.

Types of Planner People

Not all planners are created the same. There are varying degrees of people's planning tactics. Who do you most identify with?

The Master Planner - If this is you, your life is planned out to a tee. You are orderly in just about all you do, and there is likely no area of your life that does not have a carefully considered plan. You venture to know what your day, week, month, and even year looks like.

Let's Do Luncher - You don't necessarily plan out your day, your to-do list, or your projects, but you have a heavy social schedule, and like to keep track of appointments, parties, and events, especially in an effort to not double book.

Pencil Me Inner - For you, your schedule is more of a suggestion than a rule. You like to keep your life and your social calendar fluid, giving yourself the ability to be spontaneous when need be. You want options, and you like some flexibility when changes arise, and when you write things in your calendar, it will likely be in pencil.

The "I'll Get to It"

This person has a plan, even though they may not have what seems like a well-structured system like *The Planner*. They may not even write many things down. However, you can count on the fact that they will stick to their commitments. They are often more extemporaneous than the planner, but more structured than the spontaneous or eleventh-hour person.

The "Spontaneous"

"Who wants to join me on a hike this afternoon?" "It's such a nice day out, I decided to go to the beach today." "Anyone want to grab a bite to eat tonight?" These are some of the phrases that you might hear from a spontaneous person. They are famous for getting an idea and running with it. Any sort of planning happens in the moment, going where the wind takes them. Like a well-known quote from the movie, *Along Came Polly*, this person is on the "Non-plan plan." Tons o' fun! However, probably not the first pick for your team presentation or the person you'd call to help you plan an event. There is a time and a place for spontaneity, and there is a time and a place for planning.

When spontaneity is welcome:

1. Grabbing a quick bite to eat with a friend
2. Catching a last-minute show
3. Calling up a friend to see if they'd like to go on a hike
4. Asking your partner or family to go out to eat versus eating in
5. Taking a trip to the beach
6. Deciding to go to a cafe
7. Showing up to someone's house because you were in the neighborhood

When spontaneity will cause more harm than good:

1. Overseeing events (e.g., weddings, birthday parties, donation drives)
2. Putting together meetings or presentations

3. Taking someone you want to impress on a date
4. Running a business
5. Deciding to go on a vacation

The "Eleventh Hour"

This is the person who only remembers deadlines a day or so before they are due. In the workplace, they are the boss who comes up with ideas that they expect the team to implement "yesterday." This person may pop into a staff member's office with last-minute requests on a regular basis. Consistently doing things at the last minute can cause a lot of stress for everyone involved, including the person doing the last "minute-ing." If you are a person who consistently waits until things are down to the wire, you will need to expect some potential pushback and/or resentment from people around you. Over time, you will become acutely aware that by doing things at the eleventh hour, there will be many dropped balls and things falling through cracks.

PLANNING AHEAD

Contrary to what some might think about planning being too rigid, too structured or binding, planning actually frees you up, giving you peace of mind and reducing stress. It frees up your brain space from trying to remember everything on your to-do list. Once you unclutter your mind with your task list, you are now free for other activities such as creating, envisioning your next trip, and some much-needed introspection.

Planning can save you from making costly mistakes or having to retrace your steps. Planning saves you from the need to put out preventable fires, keeps you from appearing scatterbrained, and takes frantic out of the equation.

To further illustrate the importance of planning, let's imagine for a moment you have a major event on the horizon, a monumental birthday party or wedding. Could you fathom someone saying, "You know, I'm just gonna wing it. I'll let people know the date, but we will just figure everything else out the day before?" That sounds ludicrous, even for someone who flies by the seat of their pants. Situations that are not as momentous as a wedding, like job interviews, work meetings, presentations, and dinner parties, all require planning in order to be successful. Planning, wherever you fall on the spectrum, is a necessary and crucial part of life.

PLANNING FOR VARIOUS DURATIONS OF TIME

Planning will look different depending upon the variable of time in which you are planning for. For instance, planning out your year will look very different from how you plan your day or even your week. It is important to distinguish each duration of time as it relates to how we move forward within our planning and goal setting.

Year At-a-glance

Of course, it is impossible to know what a day will bring, let alone a year. Creating this type of plan is skeletal and will give you an overall framework for your bird's-eye vision of the year ahead. Yearly planning is also where you can note important dates, events, and milestones. Birthdays fit within this time frame, along with vacation dates, deciding when to start home improvement projects, the sale of your home, back-to-school days, weddings, retreats, and the like. On a business level, the yearly calendar is a good place to mark down plans for marketing, rolling out new strategies or systems, the purchase of a major software, new hires, and events. It is truly "at-a glance", and there will be limited details at this point. For this type of planning, I typically use a ***Year-at-a-Glance*** timeline (See Appendix).

The Quarter

The quarter is a great way, either in business or your personal life, to break down the year into more manageable segments. Quarters are easy to follow because they line up with the seasons, and give you a nice three-month chunk of time to attain a goal, which feels a bit more manageable than a full calendar year. Three-month segments of time are good when it comes to fitness goals, sales projections, savings plans, improving company spending, the rollout of new programs, and more. Similar to the year, the quarter is still very much an overview of what it is you hope to achieve, and it is when we get into the month, the week, and the day that the real magic happens. When planning my quarters, I sometimes use a grid-style timeline. You can find one, called the ***Quarterly Projects & Priorities Worksheet***, conveniently located in the (Appendix). It is broken down by half-year increments (Q1/Q2 & Q3/Q4).

Month At-a-glance

Most of us have the ability to look at the month ahead, whether it's on our phone or on our electronic or wall calendars. With monthly planning, it is easy to indicate items more specifically, like outings and events, birthdays, bill due dates, interviews, lunch appointments, upcoming trips, and sporting events. A month is also a good amount of time to plan a new workout regimen, small event, mini vacation, or simple home improvement project. When visualizing your month you may want to use a list-style timeline. For your convenience, I have created a ***Monthly Priorities Worksheet*** (See Appendix).

The Week

We often look at our lives in the form of a week. We ask the question, "How was your week?" Not how was your month or quarter. During the week is when we can see patterns in our lives. For instance, you may go to the gym three times a week or have a weekly call or meeting.

Each week, I choose to focus on a specific project or projects. For instance, I worked on this book for an average of three times per week, for a couple of years, until it was complete.

It's during the week that you make true progress. While we cannot control unforeseen variables, we generally have a pretty good grasp of what is on our calendar for a given week, and the targets we'd like to hit.

I personally love planning my week! This is where my day planner kicks into overdrive, taking my monthly plans and priorities, and spreading them out across seven days, making a real dent in my goals. I look at my weekly day planner multiple times per day. I can choose to look at only the current day's tasks, but also have the ability to look at the next day's plans. In case I cannot get to a task on Monday, for example, I can always move it to another day. When it comes to planning out my week, I rely heavily on my paper-based day planner. We will talk more about planning tools in a later section.

The Day

"One day at a time," "Seize the day," "Another day, another dollar." Outside of unexpected circumstances, the day is essentially the battlefield that we have the power to truly conquer. You can have a wonderfully planned-out year, month, or quarter, but it is the sum of what you do in each day of that month and year that counts. We must remind ourselves that anything worth achieving does not happen overnight. There is time necessary to make our dreams come to fruition.

I want to take this time however, to be real about this. There is nothing exciting, glamorous, or sexy about the daily plodding it takes to achieve a goal. It's often boring and sometimes grueling. Additionally, once you make it big in whatever industry or field you are trying to break into, there will be no one at the finish line to hand you a certificate of completion for all that you have done to make it there. There will be no one lauding you after looking at your daily calendar, saying, "Wow, I see now exactly what it took for you to get here."

I'll be 100% honest, there are times that I feel like pulling my proverbial hair out at the pace in which it takes to complete a project (if it takes longer than a couple of weeks). In fact, it has taken six years to complete this book, and as someone who gains a great deal of satisfaction from accomplishments, there are days I feel tortured and discouraged with the feeling that it seems like I will never be done. Then I have to remind myself about the tortoise and the hare. The hare raced through, became arrogant, and burnt out, so he decided to take a nap, but the tortoise is the one, even though it took him all day, who finished, and inevitably won the race.

If you can chip away at a project one 24-hour segment after another with steady and consistent effort, before you know it, it's been a month, or a year, and the project is complete. It's like the saying, "How do you eat a whale? One bite at a time."

PLANNING FOR VARIOUS LIFE CIRCUMSTANCES

Whether you're an entrepreneur, a student, gig worker, or a nine-to-fiver, you need to plan. That plan, however, will look different from person to person, depending upon the specifics of your life situation.

The Nine-to-fiver

While we do have 24 hours in a day, things like sleeping and getting ready in the morning must be factored in. Let's say you sleep for seven hours a night, need one hour to get ready in the morning, you have just spent eight hours of your day, which leaves a remaining 16 hours. Don't forget about that pesky little commute to and from work. For this exercise, let's say one hour. If you are one of the lucky ones who was able to maintain your work-from-home status after

COVID-19, congratulations. How could we forget about work itself? If you work a nine-to-five, that is eight to nine hours of your day.

With seven (7) hours of sleep + one (1) hour to get ready + one (1) hour of commute time + eight (8) hours of work, that equals 17 hours. You are left with seven hours in your day. Seven hours to spend however you want. You have kids, you say? Dinner time (2 hours) + homework time (2 hours) + bath time (1 hour) + bedtime (1 hour). Now, you have about one hour left to yourself. So how is it that people with children can go to school, run companies, excel at work, have time for their love lives and social lives? Planning is the key. Without it, your day can easily slip away from you. If you don't have children and a family, that opens up about six to seven hours a night during the work week, for whatever it is you want. Working out (2 hours) + dinner with friends (2 hours) + catching up on your shows (2 hours), you get the idea.

While I have spent many years as an entrepreneur, I have also spent plenty of years in a nine-to-five job. It was during those times that my nights and weekends were the way I was able to start a business, finish a novel, have a social life, take care of daily responsibilities, and pay bills.

Remember when cell phone companies would incentivize when we talked on the phone by giving us nights and weekends free? That same principle rings true for the person who works a full-time job. Nights and weekends are golden! I once told a boss who was quite the workaholic and expected the same from me, "Do you know how I am able to come back here every Monday? My nights and weekends."

The Entrepreneur

Then there are those who have decided "Nope, I am not working for someone else. I will work for myself, or I will build something and have others work for me." There is certainly a flexibility and freedom that comes with this, but unlike the person in a nine-to-five job, an entrepreneur could easily spend 12 hours of their day, 7 days per week, working on their business. While some may be able to cut out commute time, this is a very different kind of grind. The entrepreneur still has to schedule and plan. In fact, sometimes even more, since there is no one telling them what time to show up, which meetings they must attend, or when to take lunch.

It could be very easy for an entrepreneur to let time escape them, and quite possibly those 12 hours of work they may be putting in are not the most efficient use of their time, or they squander them away altogether.

Whereas someone working a nine-to-five job may need to use their nights and weekends to do some of the non-work-related tasks, for the entrepreneur, it can more easily be built into their workday, unless of course they work in a non-home based location. Nonetheless, if you are the boss, you have created for yourself more flexibility, no matter your work locale.

For me, adding non-work activities into my "work-week" provides a nice change of pace and gives my brain a break from work. However, every entrepreneur has their own rhythm. There are some who run their week much more like a nine-to-five, and they don't mix personal with business.

When I am working for myself my day looks a lot like this: Wake up sometime in the 8 or 9 o'clock hour (night owl here), do my morning rituals, including hygiene, cleaning up around the house, and making breakfast. This could take up to two hours. I generally like to exercise in the earlier part of my day, about four days per week, adding another hour-and-a-half per day. Once I have gotten all the physical activities out of the way is when I like to settle into work, whether it's writing, checking emails, making phone calls, researching, or making progress on current projects. Now it's dinner time, and I typically cook, which could take another hour to hour-and-a-half. After dinner, I normally settle back into some more writing, and by this time, it is 9 or 10 p.m. After 10 p.m. I allow myself to indulge in one or two of my favorite shows before going to bed. The measure of success for my day is whether or not I get my to-do list items accomplished. So whether I finish by 7 p.m. or 12 a.m.is simply a personal preference.

The College Student

It took me six years to get through undergrad, and after four majors, I finally figured it out, and then later went on to graduate school for two years. While I did learn a great deal in college, the necessary skills to have a successful career, I'd say college equally prepared me for life. College is truly where I learned to manage my time. Not only was I a full-time student, but I also worked part-time, throughout my entire undergraduate years, so navigating my time was dictated by whether or not I would be able to work, attend class, and have my assignments in by the due date. Ultimately, without time management, I would not have succeeded.

It was inevitable that every new semester I'd feel overwhelmed by all the assignments, readings, and test dates. My eyes glazed over as I perused each of the five to six class syllabi. How in the world was I supposed to keep all these deadlines straight? College was the first time I ever bought a day planner, the very device that literally saved my college career and my sanity.

With this small investment of money and time on the front end, all the information from the syllabi to my calendar ensured I never missed an assignment, group meeting, or test. In the standard working backwards method, I'd fill out the calendar accordingly.

I learned very quickly that college, unlike high school or elementary school, is all up to you. No one is tapping you on the shoulder, waking you up, shuttling you to class, or tracking you down when you missed a class. Just as quickly as I learned that, I realized that professors were not at all concerned with excuses for not completing an assignment on time. If you are a college student, I cannot stress enough the importance of having some type of time tracking/calendar system.

In addition to the discipline of completing assignments, I believe it is equally as important to take time to rest. In college, it's easy to blur the lines between weekdays, weekends, nights, and days. It's easy to stay up all day in class or at work, only to spend all night in the library studying, writing, and preparing. Without the proper rest, you'll burn out. My practice was to give myself one day or even just a night where I did nothing school-related. In graduate school, this was Friday night. Use this time to unwind and not think about your next assignment. Spend it with friends and family doing things that bring you the most joy and relaxation. It is so crucially important for your mental and physical health. Believe me, the paper will be there the next day.

The Parent

Parents are probably the people with the least amount of time on this whole planet. I am not a parent myself, but was the big sister to my siblings, twelve and seven years my junior. I have nannied, been the director of a youth center, and served in the teen ministry, yet I will never know the true sacrifice parents make with respect to their time. In fact, this sacrifice starts once the child is in utero, as parents prepare, plan, and rearrange their lives for their new arrival. After the baby is born, the sacrifice of time continues with sleepless nights, endless feedings, diaper changes, and the like. Once the child is in school, the splitting of time between school, homework, and extracurricular activities commences. This all happens while the parent still needs to tend to their own needs.

While working at a child development center at Cal State Long Beach, in my early 20s, there was a single mom of four girls, who I later learned became valedictorian. I was utterly shocked and amazed. Here I was, single, childless, 21, working part-time and barely scraping by with a B grade point average. What was it that this woman was doing that allowed her to be able to single-handedly raise her children, all the while breaking the glass ceiling of possibility? Even at that time in my life, I understood that she must have been an excellent steward of her time.

As a parent, it is easy to become engulfed in all that is necessary for your children, so much so that you can easily forget to tend to your own needs. While the most important role a parent will have is to help their kids to excel, it is also very important to not let go of their dreams, goals, ambitions, and purposes along the way.

The Unemployed

While this can be a trying time, and looking for a job can feel like a full-time job, this time in between jobs is rife with opportunity. Many people have started a new business during a phase of unemployment. This can also be a good time to get to know your city a little better. If you have a laptop, try rotating your time at different coffee shops, cafes, or parks, to break up the job search monotony. You never know who you will meet, and what opportunities may arise as a result. Perhaps this is also a time that you spend doing some long neglected projects, learning a new skill, catching up on reading, bumping up your workout plan.

As someone who has experienced unemployment, I would say that it is a good idea to set a routine for yourself. Perhaps, after your morning routine, you set aside a couple of hours to look for jobs, take a lunch break, and then get to it again for another couple of hours before dinner. A scheduled plan can help you avoid feeling unproductive, bored or discouraged.

The Retiree

As a retiree, you are done with work, not life! This is the time you get to use to your advantage, without the interruptions of a job! Retirement is not so unlike entrepreneurship, in that your time is your own.

For some, retirement can come as a shock, going from a full-throttle 40-hour work week to doing nothing at all. A good way to transition into this new time reality is to volunteer, perhaps at a local school, hospital or some other type of community service.

While I am not yet retired, as an entrepreneur, I know what it's like to have time on my hands, which essentially means a lot of self-management. This can unfortunately turn into what feels like a vortex of endless time, becoming rote, monotonous, boring, and unfulfilling if you don't have a goal.

My biggest suggestion for the retired individual is to have a daily and a weekly routine, something that gets you out of your pajamas. Institute a daily exercise regimen, a time of day when you focus on home projects, cleaning, errands, and appointments.

Retirement is also an excellent time to catch up on projects that you didn't have time for during your working years, like reading the books collecting dust on your shelf, spending more time with family and friends, heck, writing a book of our own.

I have a good friend who did not travel much in her younger years because she was focusing on her career, and raising a family, but as soon as she retired, boy oh boy, she puts some of us to shame with her yearly globe trotting adventures to South East Asia, the Caribbean, Europe, and Africa, and all in her 70s!

As is true for many retirees, your budget may be a large factor in determining the types of activities you can afford. Even on a budget, there are innumerable free and low cost activities in which you can partake, for instance, going on a walk, visiting a museum, spending time in nature, catching a matinee, going to a farmer's market, joining free community groups and meetups, attending a free community event, concert or festival, picnics, and the list goes on!

Enjoy this time in your life because after spending your whole life working, you've earned it!

PLAN IT AND SET IT FREE

Nothing in this life is perfect, least of all our plans. We must understand and accept that life is filled with flips and turns, many of which we cannot control. We must be nimble when it comes to our plans, otherwise, we are in for a bumpy road, fraught with irritation, frustration, and anger. Plan for what you can control, and leave space for the things you cannot.

It has taken me many years to understand this lesson. I used to be that person, irritated whenever my calendar had to change. Over the years, I have learned to allow for space within my schedule to account for unanticipated life events or mishaps. There are many factors that can arise, requiring the reorganization of your trusted calendar. Issues as simple as needing to reschedule a meeting, having a sick child, or dealing with a dead car battery, and so on.

On a grander scale, situations can shift within your organization, such as budget cuts, rebranding, or the implementation of a new program, and most of us have seen what a global pandemic can do to our plans. While changing direction can often feel painful, the best way to deal gracefully with it is to understand in the first place that nothing, truly nothing, is set in stone.

LOOKING BACK ON YOUR ACCOMPLISHMENTS

As a part of my planning, I always take time to look back on the months and weeks that have passed. I generally do this at the end of the week and the end of each month. This does a couple of things. One, as someone who likes, scratch that, loves check marks, I essentially get to see what I have achieved, creating an incredible sense of satisfaction and accomplishment. Seeing what we accomplish is especially important when tracking success because it wards off any negative messages we may tell ourselves, like, "I haven't achieved anything." or "What have I really accomplished?" The check marks do not lie. Secondly, this practice aids in planning the upcoming weeks and months, making it clear what items I was not able to get to, so that I can move them to the upcoming month and week.

In addition to looking back on my week and month, I also mark off my quarterly accomplishments. This allows me to see, on a larger scale, what I have achieved, thus heightening the sense of gratification.

Generally, it is when the month is winding down that I start to fill in the upcoming month with important projects and dates. *Note: I don't fill out the entire month with every item, but rather what I consider highly important or essential. For me, this typically means activities that will propel my goals.* Then, as the month progresses, I fill in the weeks with other daily tasks or appointments as they arise. With the exception of appointments that require specific dates and times (i.e., meetings, doctor appointments, etc.) I always keep flexibility in mind, knowing things are meant to be moved if needed (remember: pencil, pencil, pencil).

14
PLANNING PRACTICALS

Now that you have identified your priorities, it is time to plan how to execute them. In the next several pages, we will look at some practical planning tools that can help you become more efficient in your organization. In no way is this an exhaustive list, yet a sampling of practices that have proven successful in my organization journey.

PROJECT MANAGEMENT PYRAMID

In the last chapter, we discussed planning for various durations of time. In an effort to illustrate this visually, I have created the ***Project Management Pyramid*** (See table below). This tool is designed to help you to identify your most lofty (yearly) priorities/goals, and then chunk them down into bite size pieces as you slice up your year into quarters, months, weeks and days.

For example, it may be your priority to clean out your garage this year, which up until this point has seemed unimaginable. A garage filled to the brim with wall-to-wall boxes of items that you haven't seen in ages. Where do you even begin? Using the ***Project Manage-***

ment Pyramid, we will illustrate how you can tackle this major project.

Let's say there are 100 boxes in the garage, and your goal, by the end of the ***year,*** is to eliminate all of them. The next step is to break that number down into ***quarters***, 100 boxes divided by 4 quarters = 25 boxes per quarter. Or you can divide 100 boxes by 12 ***months***, which would be approximately eight boxes per month. You can further distill this down by dividing eight boxes by one month (4 weeks) = 2 boxes per ***week***. Now doesn't your project seem much more attainable when you look at it this way? No one is asking you to be a hero and try to tackle any big project in one day (remember what they say about Rome). The end goal is to get to the finish line, and if that finish line is a year away, then so be it; there is no shame in that.

This system can be used for any number of quantifiable projects, such as writing a book, and breaking down how many pages you will write per week, month or day, how many pounds you'd like to lose in a set amount of time, training for a marathon, and more. *Note:* Your goal does not need to be something that takes an entire year. You can certainly modify the system for whatever amount of time you allot for yourself, and the principles will still apply. *Try plugging one of your goals into the **Project Management Pyramid** system and watch the overwhelm melt away.*

CALENDARING & ORGANIZATIONAL DEVICES

Whether it's remembering a birthday, a work event, a pleasant lunch date, we all have things to do. If it's a paper, wall or desk calendar, a day planner, or an electronic calendar, we all need some type of system to tell us when and where we need to be. In this next section, we will discuss the most common types of calendars and effective ways for using them.

Common Organizational Devices:

1. Yearly wall/desk calendars - these are great for those at-a-glance situations, major events, standing appointments/meetings, and birthdays.
2. Day planners
3. Pen and a good old-fashioned piece of paper
4. Notebook/notepads - spiral, ledger style, bound, padded to-do list

5. Three-hole binder with paper
6. Electronic (Online) calendars (Outlook, Google)
7. Bullet journal - this is a great device for the visual person who thinks more in pictures and images than in straight lines
8. Excel spreadsheet or Word Doc

MOST COMONLY USED CALENDAR SYSTEMS

Day Planners

We have been in the digital age for many years now, and yet physical planners are still very popular. Many people, myself included, still like writing on paper. For me it is being able to touch and feel my calendar, and derive a deep sense of accomplishment and satisfaction by checking off completed tasks.

If you do use a day planner, be sure to choose one that inspires you and meets all your needs, especially since you will be committed to it for a whole year. I have used many different types of day planners, but my favorites have been the ones that have a cover that is visually appealing. I have also really enjoyed day planners with sayings, quotes, and scriptures. Lately, I am drawn to ones with fun stickers. The essentials I need from my calendar are a week-at-a-glance, month-at-a-glance, a few pages for blank notes, and a summary page that highlights goals and important dates for the month.

Throughout the weekdays, I look at my day planner at least a half dozen times a day. In the morning, I start out by looking at it to remind myself of what is on my docket for the day. I look at it again after I have completed a couple of the tasks (this creates a feeling of accomplishment). I'll look at it again after I have completed a few more tasks. Closer to the end of the day I revisit it to remind myself of what the next day will bring, and to set my wake-up alarm to align with my first morning appointment. Through the week, I am also looking several days ahead, to ensure I am on track for accomplishing those week's tasks. By the end of the week, I am planning for the week ahead. This is also the time I may move some things that I did not complete to the next week.

Electronic Calendars

The great thing about using an electronic calendar is that you can set reminders for when your meeting is approaching (the day of, and as granularly as minutes beforehand). This is good for the person who tends to run late, the forgetful soul, or the individual who gets so absorbed in what they are doing that they may need a little extra help managing their transitions.

While in my personal life I prefer paper day planners. When I was in the world of work I chose, such as Google and Microsoft Outlook. These tools are great because you can track all of your daily and monthly to-do's in one place, and what better place than to do that in the same system as your email service provider.

With electronic calendars you are able to invite people to meetings, add notes, and even cancel meetings for all invitees. They also allow for people to see available times on your calendar, to alleviate having to go back and forth in email to find common availability. In Google calendar you can have several, separate calendars that you've created, and with a simple toggle of the button those calendars will overlap so that you can see all the content in one place, and in a different color. Conversely you can choose to hide or quiet certain calendars if you do not want them visible.

Many experts believe you should only keep one calendar, and this calendar should have both your personal and business or work related items. I completely understand the wisdom behind this as it stops us from duplicating our efforts, and it also ensures you do not miss appointments. I, on the other hand, have a different thought on this. I have found that when I am working a nine-to-five job I like to keep those calendars separate from my personal calendar. What I find myself doing is keeping my electronic calendar for all work related items, and making sure that on that calendar I write in any personal appointment that may overlap or affect my work day. For instance, if I have a doctor's appointment I would add it to my work calendar. This would ensure that I didn't get so caught up in my work day that I missed the appointment.

In addition, if I had a major work event that took place outside of normal business hours I was sure to put it in my personal calendar so as not to book any personal appointments during that time. The reason for this separation of calendars for me was because when I was in the workforce I had so many meetings and tasks that it would severely overload my personal calendar if I were to use one calendar and vice versa for my work calendar. This system has worked very well for me over the years, and I have not missed appointments. However, if you choose this method, be sure to stay diligent.

MY PERSONAL PLANNING SYSTEM

Please allow me to share my system of organization and planning, which has gone through many iterations and taken many years to develop. It is not a sophisticated system in any way, shape or form, but rather the system that works best for me. I will break down each element of my system and then walk you through how I put it all together. I typically do this at the end of each year, for the upcoming year.

Journaling

For most of my adult life, I have been journaling for a variety of reasons. It is a way for me to get my thoughts on paper in a single and contained space. I use the journal to pray, to make lists, to set goals, and to flesh out my future hopes and dreams. I use the journal to recount important wisdom passed along to me by others, and I often use a journal for various forms of planning.

It is a great way to recap on the past year, to highlight my accomplishments, and to set forth the vision and themes for the year to come.

Vision Boarding

In 1997, one of my family members introduced me to vision board creation, and once I got a taste I've never looked back. I have created one every year since then. The purpose of a vision board is to create a visual representation of your goals and dreams, in order to clarify your intentions, while keeping them at the forefront of your mind.

The science supports that by regularly viewing your board, you reinforce your goals and objectives, which undoubtedly helps you stay focused and in line with your vision.

Research also states that vision boards improve goal-setting, helping individuals articulate their goals visually, which makes them more well-defined. In addition to this, vision boarding creates an alignment between your goals and values, which naturally aids in positive thinking. Finally, visual stimuli can create somewhat of a re-wiring of the brain, by a priming effect that increases one's attention to goal-related opportunities.

Creating a board is easy and fun. Simply grab several magazines and start cutting out images, words, and phrases that resonate with you. Keep in mind there is no need to have an agenda, but rather let your subconscious do the driving - if it lights you up inside, then cut it out. Once you have all the images you want, then simply use a glue stick to paste them onto a poster board (I prefer foam boards because they physically stand up on their own, and they withstand the test of time, if you choose to hang onto them for more than a year). Once it's complete, put it somewhere easy for you to see on a daily basis, and watch your goals come to fruition (even if not that year, but in years to come).

Timelining

I LOVE timelines! It is such a wonderful way to see something in its entirety, and at a simple glance. As previously discussed, this is a perfect way to get a bird's-eye view of your year, highlighting and prioritizing your most important goals.

Timelines are also an easy way to see your progress, all in one place, of the items you accomplished and those you did not. I do this by using a simple check mark to indicate what I have accomplished and putting a line through the items I did not.

White Boarding

In my office, I have a dry erase whiteboard that sits on my wall, which I use to break down my quarterly goals. I essentially take my ***Year-at-a-Glance*** timeline document and list out each quarter, one at a time, before moving on to the next quarter. Essentially, there are only ever three months at a time on the board (Q1: Jan - March; Q2: April - June; Q3: July - Sept; and Q4: Oct - Dec.) Looking at the three months at a time is a nice visual reminder that I can see whenever I walk into my office. Breaking down the quarter is a way to keep myself on track through the year, but it does not take the place of my day planner, which I use to track months, weeks, and days at a time.

Once the quarter ends, I get to put a check mark next to all the completed items, which is satisfying in-and-of-itself, and then erase that quarter, only to start afresh with the new quarter at hand. Since items on an erase board are fluid, if I want a more permanent record of the items completed, this is where the monthly (paper or electronic) calendar or ***Year-at-a-Glance*** document comes into play.

Day Planning

My day planner is the tool I use every day, and without fail. As previously mentioned, the planners I buy typically have the following components: a month-at-a-glance calendar, a summary page (which generally entails a section for monthly goals, important dates, monthly to-dos, and a section for birthdays), and most importantly, the star of the show, the week-to-week calendar, sectioned off by day.

I use the monthly-at-a-glance section of the planner for marking down birthdays, major events, deadlines, and important due dates. On the summary page, I fill in each section, specifically the goals and to-dos for that month.

Each day, within the weekly calendar section, I do a couple of things in order to be able to delineate the different types of entries. For example, if it is a meeting, phone call, or something with a specific time associated with it, I will use a visual symbol to denote that particular entry, by enveloping it in a circle, bubble or cloud so that it stands out on the page. In addition, even if there is a set time associated with a particular entry, I will rank each item with a number so that I know what will be taking place first, second, third, and so on. These visual markers help me to be able to easily identify each item without having to look too closely. For me, it is all about making my system as easy to follow as possible.

Note Taking

In addition to my day planner, I keep notes, whether electronically (on my phone), or on notepads I keep around the house. For me, notes are often lists, thoughts, notions, or reminders that are floating around in my head and need to be organized, but don't necessarily fit into the day planner; or they are thoughts I simply need to get out of my head because I am not near my planner. Some of the notes on my phone include a running list of items I need to purchase, a "Monthly Ledger," keeping track of my monthly allowance, and thoughts about my books or screenplays that I have when I am out and about.

I keep notepads around my house, as well, specifically in the nightstand near my bed, so that when a revelatory idea pops into my (theta) mind in the middle of the night or the wee hours of the morning, I can jot it down, so that I don't forget. Remember, if you think it, ink it. From the note pads, I often put the idea in the appropriate place where it lives, which is often some type of Word document. Some of the notes on my phone exist in perpetuity, and I either make check marks or delete the items once they are completed.

Color Coding

As mentioned, I have had several positions in the nine-to-five world, and when I was in those roles, I often had many spinning plates, consisting of projects, standing meetings, events, and travel. I would organize my electronic calendar by colors in an effort to make my organizational system the easiest possible. In most of my jobs, we used PC's, and Microsoft Outlook was our calendaring system.

The great thing about the Outlook calendar is that it had a function that would allow you to create a color key, whereby you could categorize your entries. For meetings, I'd use the color yellow, for events, purple, for standard to-do items, green and for urgent deadlines red. This way, when I popped into my calendar and was met with a sea of yellow, I knew I'd be in meetings for much of the day, and if the majority of the items were in green that would cue me that I'd likely be in the office much of the day, hammering out project items. Colors helped me to be able to look at my calendar, at-a-glance, and know exactly what my day entailed.

Penciling It In

While a pen is permanent, a pencil is flexible, and as we know, life is fluid, and so should your calendar be. The use of a pencil versus a pen in your calendar will help to mitigate your level of frustration when items (inevitably) change. If you look at my calendar, you can see many erasure marks from items that I've had to move around. In addition to creating a system of flexibility, pencil also alleviates the need to use white out or unsightly scratch marks.

Putting it all Together

As we looked at the several components of my organizational system, let's put it all together. I essentially use three main devices in order to keep myself on track for the year. 1) The ***Year-at-a-Glance*** timeline document (See Appendix) that I keep somewhere easy to locate (sometimes on a clipboard and sometimes on a cork board) 2) A dry-erase, whiteboard, to track my quarterly goals/targets - you can also use the ***Quarterly Projects & Priorities Worksheet*** for this (See Appendix), and 3) A day planner, where I track the monthly, weekly and daily progress of my overall goals.

At the top of the year, I fill out the ***Year-at-a-Glance*** timeline, noting all the major projects I plan to accomplish within the year. From this document, I take each quarter and put them onto a whiteboard so that I can visually track those projects in more bite-sized chunks. Alternately, you can also use the ***Monthly Priorities Worksheet*** document (See Appendix).

From the whiteboard, I then start filling out my day planner, one month at a time - first the summary page with the goals/priorities for the month, and then I plug those top priorities into each week within that month (day by day).

Note: I do not fill out my day planner for the entire year in advance, but rather one month at a time (with the exception of birthdays). Of course I will not know all of my daily appointments for the entire month, but by plugging the most important goals/appointments in advance, this keeps them from being squeezed out by other, potentially more urgent matters.

Remember to use a pencil so you can always move something if need be. Do not hold yourself to a standard of rigidity; schedules are meant to change. If you are realizing that there are some things you have yet to accomplish, just move those to weeks or months that follow.

Once the month starts to wind down, I then start to fill in the month-at-a-glance section in the day planner for the upcoming month. For more advanced planners, you may want to fill out the summary pages for an entire quarter at a time.

Principle #3 Summary

- We are naturally better with our time when we first understand what is important to us (our values and priorities).
- Everyone falls on different points on the planning spectrum. Knowing where you fall can be very helpful in learning how to become more efficient with your time.
- We all have areas in our lives that are overtaken by time bandits (whether it is too much social media or television, etc.). It is helpful to become aware of these areas so we can become more mindful stewards of our time.
- No matter what system you choose, find a time management and planning system that works best for you.
- Plans change, and are not always set in stone, be flexible and gentle when plans change, remember, pencil, pencil, pencil.

Putting Principle #3 Into Practice

1. Do you know your priorities, or do you find yourself following every whim or other people's agendas? If you find yourself struggling in this area, make a list of things that are important to you (if your list is 10 or more, try to narrow it down to 5 or fewer, and decide to focus on these areas). Take note of your productivity progress.
2. What do you value? Start by listing what is important to you when it comes to your heart, mind, body, and soul. What ideologies are you drawn to? What ignites your fire? What

do you care deeply about, and how do you like to spend your time?

3. What are some of your biggest goals? Have you focused on them or do you feel like they are slipping from your fingers?
4. Do you often feel overwhelmed by all that you need to accomplish? If so, do you have a personal time management system? Is it working for you? If not, I encourage you to find a system that works for you and stick with it.
5. Do you find yourself procrastinating when it comes to working on your goals? If so, how can you change this behavior?
6. Where do you find yourself on the *Get'er Done Continuum*? Are you satisfied with where you fall? If not, how can you gently make some shifts?
7. What are some of your time bandits? How can you mitigate how much time you lose to activities that are not getting you closer to your goals?
8. Where do you find yourself on the *Planner Spectrum*? Knowing this about yourself, are you content with your current model of planning, or can you make some adjustments?
9. What type of planning devices do you use? What have you used in the past? What has been the most effective for you? What do you think will be effective for your current goals?

Challenge:

1. Keep a ***Daily Time Log*** (See Appendix) for one week. Once the week is over look at the log and note areas or holes of time that you can be using more effectively.
2. Take a major project you'd like to accomplish and plug it into the ***Project Management Pyramid*** system, until completion.

PRINCIPLE #4: GUARDING YOUR TIME

"I must govern the clock, not be governed by it."

— GOLDA MEIR

If you don't protect your time, no one else will - not your kids, not your boss, not your spouse, not your friends or your family. In fact, those are people who will demand the most time from you, and make no mistake, people will treat you the way you allow them, and this is no different with your time. In her book, *Good Boundaries, and Goodbyes,* Lysa TerKeurst distinguishes the fact that boundaries are not for other people, but rather for your own protection.

Let's be clear, guarding your time is not synonymous with being selfish with it, it is simply creating guards around what you hold as priority in your life, and protecting yourself in a way that creates boundaries around your most precious resource, your time.

In this section, we'll take a look at ways in which you can gently put up borders in an effort to safeguard your time.

Please bear in mind that this topic resonates with me so much that I could literally write an entire book on it. For that reason, it is difficult to not to be impassioned by the subject, and frankly, a little preachy. Proceed with caution!

15
THE WAY OF THE WESTERN WORLD

"A crust eaten in peace is better than a banquet partaken in anxiety."

— AESOP

Life is not a sprint, but rather a marathon; slow and steady wins the race. Life is also not a competition about who is the MOST anything: the most disciplined, the fastest, the smartest or the richest. What life is, is about creating the most meaning possible, for yourself, and for those around you. When you embody that notion, you will find incredible freedom.

When you live a life that is simply filled with busyness, without creating real intention for your actions, you will likely be chasing your proverbial tail. Just because you are busy does not mean you are being effective. In fact, when you cut a chicken's head off, it literally runs around in circles, despite the fact that it's actually dead.

STRESSED FOR SUCCESS

If you live in the U.S. as do I, we are well-known for overworking and being overworked. The saddest part of this is that we are often applauded for working through lunch, working overtime, and not taking vacations. I'll be the first to admit I have been guilty of working through many lunches; in fact, this is part of the reason why I have so much conviction on it now. I have worked with people who prided themselves on having the cap on their vacation time because they never used it, and the way people would respond to emails on nights and weekends, you would think they were going to earn a medal. What are we trying to prove when we don't take breaks at work, don't use our vacation time, and continually work extended hours? While your workaholism may be reinforced by a bigger title, and if you're lucky a few more dollars, what is the true cost? Is a paycheck, and potentially a couple of nice words from your boss (if you have a good one), worth sacrificing your health, sanity, quality time with friends and family, and essentially your quality of life?

Where does this American mentality come from? The rest of the world, except for Japan, which rivals us in workaholism, understands that work is a means to an end. It is necessary for survival, feeding and clothing your family, and housing oneself, but it should not, and does not, define or dictate their lives.

Why is it so hard to actually put into practice terms like "Work-Life Balance," a term that has been championed by Human Resource departments to remind us to take breaks. I can't imagine anyone on their deathbed has ever uttered, "Gosh, I wish I would have worked more." What is the point of working so hard when we can't even enjoy the fruits of our labor?

Ever go away on vacation and come back to people saying how rested and radiant you look, and then by noon that glow is gone, as you have been catapulted back into the stress of your job?

After leaving a job and having been away for about a year, I went back to visit some former co-workers. One said to me, "Wow, Jennifer, you look great!" Another co-worker responded, "It's because she doesn't work here anymore."

Studies have found many health problems related to stress, which has been known to increase the risk of conditions such as obesity, heart disease, Alzheimer's, diabetes, depression, gastrointestinal problems, and asthma. Other such related diseases can include: a weakened immune response, slower healing process, sleep dysfunction, body aches, headaches, and more.

We need to ask ourselves, why are we working so hard? Don't get me wrong, I believe in hard work. In fact, I am also guilty of being a workaholic at times. I enjoy work, I gain very much pleasure from my accomplishments. In every job I have ever had, I felt like I gave it my all, and then some. What I am referring to here is balance. Any boss or company that does not respect the fact that you need time away from work (nights, weekends, lunch, vacations) is a job that genuinely does not care about your physical or mental health.

When budget cuts and layoffs occur, no decision is made to keep someone based on the fact that they worked more nights and weekends or checked more emails. The decision is made based on the company's bottom line, can they afford to keep the position or not. So ask yourself, can you afford to put your health on the line for a company that finds you dispensable?

In an article published by the Nomadx Foundation, burnout is defined as a psychological syndrome that represents a prolonged response to chronic emotional and interpersonal stressors at work. The diagnosis, which is recognized by the World Health Organization, is characterized by exhaustion, cynicism, and lack of professional efficacy. Other symptoms may include permanent tiredness, feelings of dissatisfaction, and a lack of appreciation at work. Other physical and mental manifestations of burnout include: headaches, chronic fatigue, irritability, and feelings of inability and negativity. If you are in a job that does not respect your personal time or has created burnout, perhaps it is time to find another. No job is worth losing your health, and essentially your life, over.

The moral of this story is that work is necessary, but don't let it run you into the ground. After your day is over, shut it off, spend time with loved ones, relish your weekends, take a vacation, take up a hobby, all things that are proven to increase your overall mental and physical health. Trust me, the work will always be there!

THE NINE-FIVE FALLACY

We are living in a time where people are pushing back on the notion that to be productive, one must work eight hours a day, five days a week —a model created in the early 20th century. The irony is that the 40-hour work week was fought for by labor unions, popularized by Henry Ford, and put into law in 1938, in order to protect people from overwork. It provided people with overtime pay and other labor rights. Now, over 80 years later, a system that was put in place to protect can be considered archaic, leaving people burned out and dissatisfied. There are many running jokes about the eight-hour workday, and how people probably are only really productive for about half of that time. The rest of the time is spent on texting friends, surfing the web, posting on social media, making personal calls, daydreaming, talking for extended periods of time with coworkers, or taking long breaks.

So why are American companies not following the science, which has shown that our whole way of organizing work time is unsuited for our current psychology? The countries with the highest average working hours are also the ones with the lowest productivity; conversely, those where work days are the shortest are the most productive. The science also suggests that working shorter hours each day leads to more intense and focused productivity. The ideal daily working time is around 6 hours, concentrated primarily in the morning. *Disclaimer: Your ideal time of productivity may look different from this; however, this is what research shows.*

Workers can take advantage of the hours when they are most productive, and utilize the afternoon for other activities, including social, sporting, and cultural activities. This freedom allows employees to better manage their fatigue, their work-life balance, and also allows them to engage in everyday life outside of work. Experts in psychology have shown that this way of organizing working time, short working days punctuated by short periods of vacation, is the one that makes employees happiest.

EXCHANGING HAPPINESS FOR MONEY

> *"I'd rather work in a broom closet doing what I love than a corner office doing work I hate."*
>
> — J.F. ARTHUR

So many people, myself included, have settled for the notion that the things we love have to be done outside of the regular business hours. Nights, weekends, or vacations are often when we work on our passion projects. Why have we settled for this sad "reality?" While quitting your day job to run a business, or pursue your passions may not be a luxury you have, why not choose to do work you love or at the very least enjoy? If you do have the ability to leave the job, and are done trading your time for money and the "security" of a paycheck for your entrepreneurial dream, why not?

There have been multiple times in my life that I have left a 40-hour-a-week job to pursue an entrepreneurial endeavor. Even though I was often only making enough to cover my bills, they were some of the most fulfilling and refreshing times of my life. One of those times has been while writing this book. Fairly recently, I took a day job to rebuild some capital. I had only been on the job for three months before being laid off due to COVID-19, but I'll tell you this, that day was one of the happiest days of my 2020. It was during this job, which was a far cry from fulfilling, that I made a solid resolution, from that point on, I needed "My passions and my paycheck to intersect!" Whether you are a business owner or you work for someone else, it is essential for your sanity that you do something that brings you joy.

TAKE YOUR TIME

Unless it is a work deadline or other specific project that requires your immediate attention, your time is yours, and you can take as much of it as you want. If you want to take six months to read a book that someone else can finish in a day, that is up to you. Do you like long baths as part of your self-care routine? Do it. Maybe it takes you longer to understand complicated problems or you need some reflection before committing to a major decision. At the end of the day, your time belongs to you. Don't let other people rush you through your process or your life.

If it is appropriate and does not disturb someone else's goals or progress, then take all the time you need. Going through a breakup, and someone says, "Just get over it already." Nope, you don't get to make that decision for me. Making a big purchase and the salesperson says I need your decision by today? Sorry buddy, you will have to wait (and if they want the sale, they will). The essence is that we all move at different paces, and we must not let other people's impatience or discomfort rush us through our necessary processes.

16
THE POWER OF YOUR WORDS

"There is no greater fraud than a promise not kept."

— GAELIC PROVERB

THE POWER OF SAYING 'NO'

My mom has been known to use a colloquialism or two. When I was younger, she used one in particular, which quite frankly annoyed me, and most of the time I ignored it, despite the frequency of hearing it, "You can't dance on every set." This, over the years, has been hard for me, since as a young person I often had FOMO (Fear of Missing Out).

The same quote that used to grate on me has now become something I hold dear. I no longer want to have so much going on in my life that I barely have time to breathe. The power of not feeling guilty when you say no is a wonderful and freeing feeling. I must say, as women, we probably struggle with this more than our male counterparts. We often have the desire to please, to be liked or to not let people down. I have had to work hard to not only protect my time from others' agendas, but also to guard my heart and spirit from feeling guilty when saying no.

In habit three, "Putting First Things First" of the *7 Habits of Highly Effective People*, Stephen's son, Sean Covey recaps that, "The key to saying no is having a deeper yes burning inside of you."

I have a dear friend who had a hard time saying "no." The way she crammed her day made me look like a lazy slouch. The saying, "You can't dance on every set," had yet to be introduced to her because she would literally show up to every party and engagement that was happening around her. While I believe she felt like she was doing a service to those she showed up for, it felt the opposite to be on the receiving end. Her stopping by a birthday party or important event for 30 to 40 minutes didn't really make me feel special. In fact, I would rather she didn't show up at all. Perhaps this is my all-or-nothing nature speaking, but it felt like a let-down. While I appreciated her showing up, the disappointment I felt when she abruptly left was not worth the short-term joy I had for her brief presence. We are busy people, and sometimes we need to split our time, but it is also okay to tell someone you won't be able to make it to their party because you have a prior commitment.

The above example may seem like a frivolous complaint, but consider if you had so much on your plate as a professional that you only showed up 75% of the way for your clients, team or company. How would your staff feel? Would you be able to keep your job if you only completed 65% of your assignments? What about if you had too many clients to juggle, causing you to drop balls all over the place?

The point is this, the only way to be good at all the "yeses" is to only say "yes" to a few things, and do them well. There have been many parties, concerts, events, or other gatherings I have turned down when I was in a period of intense focus. In fact, it was while I was in grad school that I started to grasp the power of saying "no." If I had not, I would have essentially flunked out of school, having squandered tens of thousands of dollars. How absurd I would have sounded, telling a professor the reason I did not finish my assignment is because I did not set strong enough boundaries with my friends and family or because my social calendar was just too full.

The ability to set strong boundaries comes in handy under numerous circumstances. Perhaps you are studying for a certification, have a writing goal, learning a new sport, taking time for your mental health, caring for your body by going to the gym, or devoting more time to your family.

Boundaries are in no way meant to be about "me, me, me," or an excuse for hoarding your time. They are also in no way a means for shirking your responsibilities or obligation to help someone in genuine need. I am also not advocating that we simply say "no" because we don't *feel* like doing something. There are many things in life we do, despite not feeling like it. This is called sacrifice, and we do this for the people we care about. What I am referring to is saying "no" to that which is extraneous ("extra-curricular"). Creating boundaries is about prioritizing what is most important to you, and counting all else as secondary.

Another time I found myself saying "no" was when I was focused on my novel. There were so many events and activities that I wanted to participate in, but I had to discipline myself for that period of time in order to meet my own personal deadlines. To this day, I cannot tell you the actual activities I "missed out on," but what I can tell you is the immense personal satisfaction that came from publishing my first book!

If you are accustomed to saying "yes" most or all the time, this is going to be a challenging task. It will not feel comfortable at first, and you may undoubtedly feel like you are being mean or unloving, but I guarantee you, the people to whom you say no will understand.

They will find someone else to babysit, run the event, take them to the airport, or do that project or task. However, if you continue to silently suffer your way through life, by saying yes to everyone, you will likely face exhaustion, illness, burnout, or even bitterness.

When I say "no", it does not mean I don't love you or that you are not important to me. It also does not mean I don't want to spend time with you. However, it does mean that there is something I may need to do that comes as a priority. If we said yes to everything, we'd never do any one thing well.

In the beginning, saying "no" may feel very strange. If you are not in the habit, it will not easily roll off your tongue. One thing you can do is practice saying it aloud, and even look at yourself in the mirror to start to become comfortable.

<u>There are many ways to say "no," without saying N-O. Try some of these phrases on for size:</u>

1. My plate is a bit too full right now for that.
2. If this is something that can wait (fill in the time frame) then I'd be more than happy to do it.
3. Unfortunately, that project is not in line with my current life goals.
4. That project/task/assignment is out of the scope of my abilities or skill sets (Let's be real. Some of us have said yes to things that truly are out of our purview because we don't want to disappoint).
5. Unfortunately, I'm going to have to pass, but have a great time.
6. I wish I could, but I already have plans.
7. *If it's a last minute request:* I wish I would have known about this sooner, but I already have plans.

8. I'm really flattered that you would think of me. Unfortunately, I don't have the bandwidth for that at this time.
9. Unfortunately, I am unable to at this time; will there be another opportunity for this in the future?

Before Making Commitments

There is nothing wrong with saying to someone, let me get back to you on that. In fact, you may want to consider this as a general practice.

Before saying yes to a request, ask yourself these key questions:

1. *If it is a major project:* Does it fit in with my personal mission/life goals and core values?
2. *If it is a smaller task:* Ask when the person may need it, then ask yourself, does it fit into my calendar.
3. *If it requires money:* Check with your budget and/or your life partner.
4. *If you are guided by your faith:* Pray about it, and ask for it to become evident if this is something you should be spending your time doing.

When you are tempted to impulsively say yes, ask yourself some of these questions:

1. Am I only saying yes because I want this person to like me?
2. Do I want to make some extra money even though I know it may be at the expense of my family, physical or mental health?
3. Do I simply not want to let this person down?

4. Do I want to avoid looking selfish?
5. Am I doing this out of guilt or compulsion?
6. What would be the worst thing that could happen if I said no?
7. Is this commitment going to cause strife or added strain in the most important relationships in my life (e.g., spouse, children)?
8. If I say no, do I think they may never ask me to do anything else again?
9. If I say yes, am I going to regret it?

If you answered yes to any of the above questions, you may really want to consider using some of the NO statements we discussed in the above section. Otherwise, you may be causing yourself unwanted grief.

The beautiful thing is, it's your life, and you get to ***choose*** what you do with it, and how you spend your time is most certainly part of that choice.

LET YOUR YES BE YOUR YES

As much as we need to set healthy boundaries and learn the art of saying "no", there are many situations in which we say "yes." The most important point here is that when saying "yes," we now have the responsibility to follow through, so don't use this word lightly. Sometimes we say yes to avoid conflict, but have no intention of following through. However, mindlessly saying "yes" is a risky game, especially if you do not keep your commitment. People will perceive you as unreliable and will be unable to trust you. Unforeseen circumstances arise, and sometimes we cannot make commitments as a result of them. If you want to be known as someone with integrity and who can be trusted, then be sure to communicate with people when and if you are unable to make your commitments.

One of my favorite stories about having integrity is a parable in the Bible about a father who asked both of his sons for a favor. The first son said, "No, I cannot do that," and the second son said "Yes." The son who said "no", ended up actually doing what his father asked of him, and the son who said "yes", did not. The question is this. Which son was the obedient one? The answer, the son who said "no", and later did it.

This parable does not go into depth about the intentions or motivations of the sons; we can only speculate. Maybe the son who said yes was simply placating his father in order to avoid conflict. Or perhaps he had every intention of doing the task, but forgot. Quite possibly, he just got busy and didn't have the time, after all. Whatever his reason, the fact remains that he did not honor his word. His "yes" was not his "yes." This can easily become a habit for us, especially living in a world so demanding of our time.

If you decide to move forward with a commitment, be sure to add it to your calendar or wherever you keep reminders so that you will not forget to uphold your promise.

SETTING TIME LIMITS

As we have discussed, setting boundaries is not code for not helping, serving or otherwise being available for people. However, it is more than alright when you show up for people to set time limits.

For example, let's say you have committed to helping a friend move, and you have determined that you have four hours available for this. Instead of your friend assuming you are free all day, you should let them know this time limit. This will be beneficial for the both of you.

By being up front with your time limit, this will alleviate the feeling of your whole day being monopolized, and it will help to set the expectation in your friend's mind, so they are better prepared, and know how to best utilize your help. If this time limit is not set, they could easily assume you are free all day, leaving you in a position to explain why you need to leave. Doing this up front will eliminate any awkwardness, miscommunication, or failed expectations.

17
REST & REJUVENATION

"People who cannot find time for recreation are obliged sooner or later to find time for illness."

— JOHN WANAMAKER

THE POWER OF REST

Sadly, resting is not the American way, terms like, "Work hard, play hard," and "It's all about the grind," are all too familiar in our society. With a measly 2 weeks (10 days) of standard vacation time per year, the go, go, work, work mentality is perpetuated at the corporate level. In many countries, outside the U.S., there is a much better balance of work and life, with many places offering a standard of six weeks vacation, siesta, and other ways that allow for respite.

While working on the set of a television show as a background actor, I casually chatted with one of the crew members and learned more about his role. He told me he worked on average about 14-hour days, five days a week. I remarked that he must be able to take some nice vacations with the money he makes. What he said next startled me, "I'll rest when I die." He was dead serious (pun intended). I thought to myself that it may be sooner than you think. It took everything in me not to lecture this 60-year-old man. In actuality, he was probably in his 50s, but he looked so haggard and worn that it was hard to tell. He smelled of cigarettes, with huge bags under his eyes, dry skin, and a pot belly. He looked absolutely exhausted. I walked away feeling very sad and thought, what is the point of all that work if you can't even enjoy the fruits of your labor?

For many years, I had no earthly idea how to relax, and often struggled with the concept of having down time. I was constantly going and doing, never any time to be still. I was of the mind that if I wasn't "being productive" I was wasting time or being lazy. Whether it was going to school, going to the gym, going to a party, going on a trip, I was on the go! I would inevitably wear myself out to the point of getting sick, at which point I was forced to sit still, but once I was better, it was "Go-go Gadget Jen," all over again.

In the course of my nine-to-five work, I held two jobs where I worked straight through the day with no significant breaks. At both of those jobs, I became overweight and was told by my doctor that I had a vitamin D deficiency because in the 5.5 years, I could literally count on one hand how many times I actually stepped away from my desk. Believe it when I say not one of my supervisors ever lauded me for my dedication to eating lunch at my desk.

Humans are finite creatures. Finite in years, and also finite in the amount of strength and energy we can expend on a daily basis. Pilots are restricted to a certain number of hours they can work in a day, a week, a month, and even a calendar year, and aren't you glad about this? Nobody wants a sleepy pilot in the cockpit. While nurses often work 12-hour shifts, they generally don't do this for more than three to four days per week. Ever pull an all-nighter for school or work?

How was that for you? I spent six years in undergrad, and two years in grad school, and I pulled a grand total of one all-nighter. Hard to believe, right? It's because it was such an awful experience that I vowed never to repeat it again.

We need time to rejuvenate, reflect, recharge, reinvigorate, recuperate, and R-E-S-T. Taking a break, even if only for a short period, can provide the rejuvenation you need. Rest is for both our bodies and our minds. It has been scientifically proven that breaks restore mental and physical energy, increase productivity, enhance creativity, reduce stress, improve mood and decision-making, boost your immune system, and can essentially add years to your life. Take lunch, take your vacation, it is part of your benefits package, and if we must go there, it's the *law* in most workplaces.

If resting is not something you are used to, it could really take some time for it to become a habit. Believe me, when it does, you will be hooked.

If we are run down and burned out, we are no good for anyone else. Rest prepares you to get up and get back out there, serving people, loving your family, being a great friend, employee or parent. If you are an empty vessel, you will have nothing in you to give. However, if you get the necessary rest, you can refill your tank, which will allow you to continue to give of yourself. With rest comes many benefits, and without it many detriments.

Getting sufficient rest has so many long-term and short-term benefits. Relaxation helps your body repair itself, which directly and positively affects your immune system. In the next section, we will discuss, in length, some of these benefits.

THE BENEFITS OF REST

Much like the fact that we must eat food and drink water to survive, and exercise to keep fit, rest is essential in the equation for keeping a healthy mind, body, and existence.

Rest activates the parasympathetic nervous system - the opposite of the sympathetic nervous system, which is the fight-or-flight response created by stress, and an unavoidable part of life. These stress hormones produce cortisol, which make you feel panicked and on edge.

Studies have shown that chronic stress suppresses our immune system and increases risk of disease. So when we take the time to recharge and ***reduce stress,*** we're not only helping ourselves physically by reducing the risk of potentially fatal health issues, but we also improve our mood.

In addition to being great for our bodies, rest is for our minds as well. Our brains are much less functional when fatigued. Our most productive times are generally after an extended period of rest. Think about how much more productive you feel on a Monday morning, after you've had a couple of days of rest, versus on a Friday after a long workweek. Rest provides a rejuvenated and refocused mind. Taking time out to recharge and declutter our minds by providing quiet moments of reflection can ***improve creativity,*** often resulting in breakthroughs and increased problem-solving abilities.

Working too long, without breaks, stifles concentration and can deplete our emotional capacity. Taking regularly scheduled breaks allows us to refresh our perspective, which in turn helps us to ***make better decisions.*** The term "sleep on it" exists because rest improves this ability.

Something that often gets lost and overlooked in our busy Western society is the need for relationships. Have you ever asked a friend to spend time, but can never seem to link up because you are both so busy? By setting aside at least one restful day per week to devote to the people in your life, you will both ***strengthen and deepen your relationships.***

When we are running mock ten, with our hair on fire, we rarely have to take care of ourselves. Rest gives us the much-needed ***times of reflection*** necessary to get a bigger picture perspective on our lives. These times help to provide clarity as we evaluate if we are on the right path with respect to our values and priorities.

Choosing time to rest from your work, and establishing an identity outside of your occupation helps to foster a more well-rounded self, thus creating harmony and balance in your life.

Emergencies and crises are a part of life, and none of us is exempt to trials. By giving yourself much-needed rest you will be better ***equipped*** *(mentally, physically, and emotionally)* ***to handle emergencies*** as they arise.

Rest does not happen by accident, but rather, you must be intentional as you fold it into your everyday life. Pencil it into your calendar, schedule a date with yourself, and make it happen!

TYPES OF REST

We all have different requirements for rest, depending on our individual needs. Good thing rest comes in many forms. We can rest while we sleep, as well as when we're awake. Below are various types of rest and restful techniques you can add to your life as a daily or weekly practice.

Breathing

It is something we do involuntarily, and it is the source of our life. There have been innumerable studies and articles published around the importance of intentional breathing as it relates to rest, relaxation, and peacefulness in our bodies and minds.

When we feel fear, pain, or intense discomfort, our breathing speeds up and becomes more shallow, igniting our sympathetic nervous system, which is responsible for the body's stress responses, and this can often lead to panic attacks.

On the contrary, when we are feeling safe and at rest, our breathing slows and deepens because we are under the influence of the parasympathetic nervous system. Slow and deep breathing increases the activity of our vagus nerve, a part of this same system. This nerve is responsible for controlling and measuring the activity of a number of our internal organs. When the vagus nerve is stimulated, it creates a sense of calm throughout the body. Our heart rate slows, blood pressure decreases, and our muscles begin to relax.

Deep breathing is a healthy, natural and safe way to find psychological and physiological relief. The benefits of deep breathing are numerous, including ***stress relief,*** resulting in a calmer and more focused mind state. In general, paying attention to our breath diverts our attention from our problems or fears to that of the breathing, which naturally helps us to be more mindful and calm. By devoting only a few minutes each day by finding a quiet spot to focus on breathing we can better manage our symptoms and achieve a better sense of calm in our daily lives.

When we are tense and stressed, it can exacerbate the body's ***pain response,*** and deep breathing can help to reduce this pain because it also causes our body to release endorphins, the chemicals in the brain that help us feel good. Endorphins play a crucial role in decreasing pain perception.

Breath control also positively impacts our ***immune system.*** This occurs specifically because deep breathing helps to oxygenate our blood supply to our veins. Oxygenated blood transports vital nutrients more efficiently, allowing our bodies to maximize these vitamins, an essential process for building immunity, in addition to ***increased levels of energy*** and ***feelings of alertness.***

Deep breathing has been proven to improve how our bodies respond to the demands of exercise. Not only does it help our body to be more accustomed to intense workouts, it also reduces the chances of injury by training our body to have a ***quicker recovery time.***

One very essential deep breathing benefits is a healthier heart rate, which directly contributes to ***lower blood pressure***. Breathing deeply helps our muscles to relax, which allows the blood vessels to dilate, stimulating circulation. Enhanced circulation is essential to decreasing blood pressure, enabling a calmer, more centered feeling.

Breathing deeply also helps train our core muscles. Keeping this part of our body strong is essential to ***improving overall balance and stability***, which have a direct effect of strength that is necessary for engaging in both sports and other everyday activities.

There are several different methods for focused, deep breathing. Some key techniques include ***good posture***, which is very important for breathing. Be sure to hold yourself upright, with your shoulders back, whether sitting or standing. Good posture facilitates the free flow of the respiratory muscles (diaphragm).

While you breathe, ***observe your respiratory movements*** - taking note of each inhalation and exhalation. You will want to focus on the sensations you feel as air passes through your nose and throat, in addition to the movements of your chest and belly. When you feel your thoughts adrift, which is completely normal, try your best to redirect your mind to your breathing.

One form of deep breathing is called ***abdominal breathing***, or breathing through your stomach. You can start by inflating your belly by inhaling, as if filling it with air, then swell your chest as you exhale. First "empty" your stomach, then your chest. This type of breathing is better done lying down with one hand on your stomach.

Rhythmic breathing entails a pause of airflow. For instance, near the end of each inhale, pause briefly while holding the air and mentally counting to three before exhaling. This pause and counting can also be done after exhaling. This technique is especially beneficial for those who deal with anxiety because it further increases slow breathing, which is important for calming anxiety attacks.

Another known technique is to ***alternate nostrils*** while breathing. This entails breathing in and out slowly through one nostril, holding the other one closed with your finger. Reverse and continue by alternating regularly. The research suggests that breathing through the nose is more soothing than breathing through the mouth.

Finally, the way to make the most of your deep breathing exercise, whichever you choose, is to ***think positive and reassuring thoughts*** while breathing. For example, with each breath, imagine you are inhaling calm, peace, joy, and when you exhale, you are getting rid of stress, anxiety, and fear.

Waking Rest

In many cultures, morning is a time for important rituals and resetting your mind to successfully tackle the day. Exercising, taking walks, or even sitting for morning coffee or tea.

However, if you are like many people in a high-performance society, starting their day by shooting out of bed like a cannon, not able to rest again until bedtime, then try this relatively new technique called *waking rest.*

Waking rest is the act of remaining awake while unassigned to any particular task. It's a period of calm, meditative thought at which your brain is able to process thoughts that arise spontaneously, much like traditional rituals of meditation. It's a time of distraction-free and reflective thought, which requires no forced efforts.

It can be achieved simply by sitting or lying quietly. It is best performed in the morning right after waking up, when your mind is still in its theta state. Anywhere from five to 20 minutes can suffice. This practice can be instituted several times a day in an effort to recenter yourself.

Down time

We all have natural lulls in our days. Times in which not much is happening. It may not be a long duration, but if you look for it, you can guarantee that you can find little nuggets of unutilized time. As we discuss the notion of rest, it is important to use this time to regroup. This can be a time when you do something you enjoy, something that fills your cup, or simply time to chill.

Down time can be those few minutes after you put your baby down for a nap, time in between meetings, or time before your next destination. If you have more time than just a few moments, this would be a great time to really invest in your mental and physical health by practicing waking rest or indulging in something a bit more extravagant, like a bubble bath or a massage. You can use your down time for something as simple as sitting and staring out the window, daydreaming about your next vacation. Perhaps you use the time to stretch or catch up with a friend. Choose what works best for you, and be sure to choose something that allows you to pause, breathe, and be.

Self-Compassion

Over the years we have heard terms such as *Self-care,* the action and approaches that embody being kind and considerate to oneself, and *Self-love,* which can take on many different forms, and in some cases, it can mean doing the inner-work and diving deep into what makes us tick.

One study showed that *self-compassion* cultivation may be helpful for improving such areas of our lives as compassion toward others, mental health resilience, and burnout prevention.

Expert, Kristin Neff explains that having self-compassion builds resiliency against depression and anxiety, while increasing life satisfaction, optimism, social connectedness, and happiness.

In the realm of rest, self-care, self-compassion, and self-love can happen in minutes within your day, and be as small as taking a moment to get up from your desk to grab a snack or stare out the window, or it can be as involved as taking a month-long sabbatical from your work.

Self-compassion can also show up by choosing to be kind to yourself rather than harshly judging every mistake you make, or refraining from believing the negative tapes we can often play in our heads. Try forgiving yourself when you make errors, and see how differently you feel. This practice will not only work for you, but will inevitably transfer to how you treat others, and we can all use a little more grace.

<u>Other ways to recharge and rest:</u>

1. Take in the nature (beach, mountains, sunsets, stargazing, bird watching)
2. Meditate
3. Swim
4. Go Dancing
5. Take a walk
6. Go for a bike ride
7. Have a meal with friends & family
8. Sit in the sauna or hot tub
9. Get a massage
10. Listen to music
11. Take a bath or shower
12. Read (including audio books)
13. Watch a favorite show or movie
14. Sit or lie on the beach
15. Journal

16. Have a picnic
17. Fly a kite
18. Go on a vacation
19. Attend a sporting event
20. Stretch or do yoga
21. Take up a hobby

THE SIGNIFICANCE OF SLEEP

Sleep is the big sister of rest, and is a crucial role in determining our quality of life. While we sleep, our bodies work to support and strengthen many key bodily functions, and without it there are many adverse effects.

According to the CDC, most people will begin to experience the effects of sleep deprivation after just 24 hours, claiming that staying awake for at least 24 hours is comparable to having a blood alcohol content (BAC) of 0.10. In the U.S., it is illegal to drive with a BAC of 0.08 or above.

The effects of going without sleep for 24 hours can include things such as drowsiness, irritability, difficulty remembering, reduced coordination, impaired judgment, increased blood sugar levels, muscle tension and a higher risk of accidents.

In a separate research study conducted by the U.S. Centers for Disease Control and Prevention, one in three American adults do not get sufficient sleep, and one of the most serious issues connected to this is an increased amount of stress. Getting quality sleep can help regulate and reduce the production of cortisol, which is the hormone connected to stress.

Sleep deprivation also disrupts the body's natural sleep-wake cycle, which affects hormones that regulate growth, appetite, metabolism, and the immune system. The effects of sleep deprivation intensify the longer one is awake. After 48 hours without sleep, a person's cognitive performance will worsen, and they will become very fatigued. At which point, the brain will start to enter brief periods of complete unconsciousness, also known as microsleep, which occurs involuntarily and can last for several seconds.

After 72 hours without sleep, deprivation symptoms and fatigue will intensify even further, having a profound effect on one's mood, cognition, and reaction times, which can result in extreme fatigue, difficulty multitasking, severe concentration and memory issues, paranoia, depressed mood, and difficulty communicating with others.

People who lack sleep also run a greater risk of contracting colds and infections. Studies have also shown that not getting enough quality sleep can lead to decreased ability to respond to insulin, increased food consumption, especially fatty, sweet, and salty foods, and decreased physical activity. All of these factors can contribute to obesity and other chronic and serious illnesses such as type two diabetes, high blood pressure, heart disease, stroke, and early death.

Sleep and mental health are interchangeable. Research has shown that one night of sleep deprivation can dramatically affect mood. Chronically experiencing poor sleep quality can be linked to depression and anxiety, which can have a bidirectional effect, meaning you get poor sleep, which causes depression and anxiety, which can cause sleeplessness, and the vicious cycle continues.

PRACTICING PROPER SLEEP HYGIENE

Most adults need anywhere between seven to eight hours of sleep each night to function optimally, and creating good habits of sleep hygiene can help to optimize sleep and restfulness. Sleep hygiene essentially is the environmental, behavioral and physiological factors that aid in better sleep.

Signs of poor sleep hygiene may include having difficulty falling asleep, experiencing frequent disturbances during sleep, and struggling with fatigue during the day. In addition, a lack of consistency in sleep quantity and quality is a tell-tale sign of poor sleep hygiene.

Sleep hygiene hinges mostly upon what we do before bedtime. If you don't already, try adding some of these practices into your daily routine: being physically active, exposing yourself to sunlight and restricting your in-bed activities - meaning, with the exception of sex, sleep should be the only use of your bed. This will train your brain to know that this is a place of rest.

While adding methods to your daily regimen is important for sleep hygiene, equally there are some habits we should also eliminate or decrease. For instance, it is best to reduce screen time close to your bedtime. Evidence has shown that screen use just before bed may impact sleep because of the blue light that is emitted from the device, which can affect the production of magnesium, the hormone necessary for the body to fall asleep. Other reasons include the content that we may be consuming on screen. If you watch a scary movie, read an emotionally charged article, or any other anxiety-provoking content, it can affect your ability to fall asleep. Sleep experts suggest putting away all screens at least one hour before bedtime. You can replace this with some light reading or another relaxing activity.

Similarly, alcohol consumption too close to bedtime, while it may help a person fall asleep quickly, is known to hinder the quality of sleep, quite often causing interruptions. In this vein, also refrain from drinking caffeine too close to bedtime. Additionally, consuming large meals near bedtime can cause sleep interruptions or trouble falling asleep. If you choose to consume alcohol, caffeine or large meals, it is best done several hours before bedtime, in order to give it ample time to be released from the system.

For us night owls, it is a good idea to give yourself some lead time in order to wind down from whatever activities you are partaking in close to bedtime. One method I use is setting a bedtime alarm on my phone. This alerts me that it is time to start wrapping up whatever I am doing and begin my nighttime rituals. In addition, establish a realistic bedtime and stick to it every night, even on the weekends.

One key element of sleep hygiene, beyond simply our habits, is the environment in which we sleep. Your room should be calm and free from disruptions, like a blaring television. Your mattress and pillow should be comfortable for your body. Be sure your sheets and blankets line up with your preferences. Controlling the temperature of your space is also highly important for optimal sleep; too hot or too cold may cause disruptions. You can implement the use of dimmer lights near bedtime in order to increase the production of magnesium, which aids in sleep. Use blackout curtains or an eye mask to prevent light pollution, and if you live in an area that is filled with excessive external noise, use earplugs, a white noise machine, or a fan to drown out those unwanted sounds.

Some other methods and natural remedies for falling asleep include using meditation and mindfulness practices like deep breathing that can put you in the proper sleep mindset.

If you have instituted the above-mentioned methods, but are still having some difficulties you can try some natural remedies like camomile tea, tart cherries or tart cherry juice, or magnesium supplements.

All in all, sleep hygiene is a multilevel approach. If you are someone who finds it difficult to get a full night's rest, try implementing some of the practices mentioned.

THE POTENT LITTLE POWER NAP

The debate has raged for years about whether or not you can make up for sleep, and some experts believe you can, citing that our bodies operate on a weekly sleep cycle. Stating that we need thirty-five 90-minute cycles per week, or an average of 7.5 hours per day. The notion is that as long as you get the full amount of sleep required during the week, you can sleep less or more on any given day, as long as it adds up to the necessary weekly requirements. I have personally put this theory to the test and have seen the evidence of its effectiveness. While we cannot replace nightly sleep, naps are a great stop gap. Instead of opting for "fake-awake" by dowsing ourselves with caffeine or lab-engineered energy drinks when we feel drained, unmotivated, and lethargic, why not try a nap instead, and give your body what it is actually craving, sleep.

I am a strong believer in naps and have been partaking in them since I was in college. In undergrad, when I was feeling run down, I'd go to the music listening lounge and pull up a bean bag, or I'd use my backpack as a pillow on the grassy knoll, or even a stack of books in the library to indulge in a 5 to 20 minute snoozefest. When I entered the world of work, I'd often eat lunch at my desk, and then use the remaining time to recline in my car for a blissful slumber. Whether it was 20 or the full 45 minutes, I'd wake up feeling refreshed and ready to take on the second half of my day. For me, naps are highly effective little oases of magical refreshment in the middle of my day, as I have seen the proof of their effectiveness for resetting my body and mind.

Your power nap doesn't have to look like mine. Find a system that works best for you, but if you haven't before, give it a try. Who knows, you may even save a few dollars on all that afternoon caffeine.

Benefits of Napping

Let's be clear, naps are meant to provide a temporary refreshment, whereas sleep provides complete physical replenishment. The most notable difference between napping and sleeping includes duration and sleep cycles. During sleep, your brain moves through four stages. The stages progress through light sleep, deep sleep, and REM cycles, which repeat for 90-110 minute intervals.

Knowing that napping does not replace sleep, there are still many benefits, including relaxation and reduced fatigue. Studies show that people who take afternoon naps wake up with a similar energy they would get from consuming caffeinated beverages or energy drinks. A separate study conducted at NASA surveyed the cognitive effects of napping on military pilots and astronauts. Those who took a nap improved overall performance by 34% and alertness by 100%.

On a mental level naps improve our alertness, boost cognitive flexibility, memory and improve focus. Physical benefits of napping include improved overall physical performance, reduced muscle soreness, better heart health, and faster reaction time. Naps, along with proper nighttime rest, have also been known to reduce impulsivity, boost productivity, and decrease irritability.

Drawbacks of Napping

While there are many benefits to napping, we know there is always a flipside. That's life, right? One such drawback of napping is that it cannot replace our nightly sleep needs, and there are many people who are not able to nap, primarily because they wake up feeling groggy. If napping seems to be getting in the way of you capturing your nightly rest, you should try to remove them from your daily schedule. For this reason, there are rules to napping that are best when followed. A good rule of thumb is to only nap when you really feel like you need some extra energy; otherwise, you can possibly disrupt your night's sleep. If you experience insomnia or poor night's sleep, napping might worsen these problems. In addition, long or frequent naps may interfere with nighttime sleep.

Best Methods for Napping

As we have already discussed, true sleep occurs within the deep sleep and REM stages, during which your body undergoes the most impactful restoration. Again, experts recommend that adults get between 7 to 9 hours of sleep every night to maintain a healthy, high-functioning lifestyle.

The ideal nap length depends on a few different factors: how much time you have to sleep, how soon you need to feel increased alertness after your nap, and how long you want that energy boost to last. A short nap is ideal when you need an immediate shot of energy to get through your work day, while a longer nap is better if you find yourself or foresee experiencing sleep deprivation.

According to the National Sleep Foundation, the best nap lengths for adults are either 20 or 90 minutes. Ten to 20-minute naps, also referred to as power naps (or cat naps), allow you to wake up feeling refreshed, energized, and alert, and will have little to no impact on your nighttime rest. The 90-minute nap allows you to cycle through all sleep stages. However, naps longer than 30 minutes but shorter than 90 may instigate the phenomenon called sleep inertia, in which one feels confused or groggy upon waking. Similarly, napping too close to bedtime may cause difficulty sleeping at night. For this reason, do your best to schedule your nap several hours before you plan to go to bed, ideally in the early afternoon as naps after 3:00 p.m. can interfere with nighttime sleep.

Other Tips for Effective Naps

Much like sleep hygiene practices for your nightly routine, nap in a quiet, calm, dark place with a comfortable room temperature and few distractions or sounds. One of the most challenging parts of napping can be falling asleep. If you find yourself having trouble dozing off, consider using a weighted blanket. You may also consider practicing mindfulness techniques or applying balms or essential oil blends for sleep.

If, however, you don't actually fall asleep, don't fret, all is not lost. You might still reap the benefits from quietly resting. Researchers have found that what they call "napitation", a brief nap or meditation, can slow brain waves and result in similar levels of regenerative rest as a nap.

Setting an alarm for your naps is a must, especially if you're not used to taking them. This will help to ensure you stay within the recommended nap lengths. Also, be sure to consider how long it takes you to fall asleep and factor that into your alarm setting.

After napping, give yourself time to wake up before resuming activities — particularly those that require a quick or sharp response.

TAKING BREAKS

We have discussed many aspects of rest and rejuvenation. One that is looked upon in the Western World of work as a villain of productivity is the break. Why is this such a bad word? I believe it goes back to our belief in the U.S. that working hard means you run yourself into the ground, when in actuality, research has proven that taking regular breaks throughout your workday creates even more effective and efficient workers.

According to an article published by Fast Company, synthesizing the research of several experts, breaks should not be thought of in terms of a set number per day, but rather, breaks should be taken every 75 to 90 minutes. Tony Schwartz, the founder of the Energy Project, calls this work-and-break pattern "Pulse and Pause." His research shows that humans naturally move from full focus energy to physiological fatigue every 90 minutes. This number was derived in part based on the productivity of musicians' durations of effective practice, in addition to the average college class duration.

Working for 75 to 90 minutes takes advantage of the brain in two different modes, learning and focusing. When one completes a task followed by a 15-minute break, the brain has time to consolidate and retain information.

An experiment by the software startup Draugiem Group used a time-tracking app and learned that the most productive workers took regular and frequent breaks, averaging working 52-minute sprints with 17-minute breaks. These particular employees achieved more in these so-called work "sprints" because they worked with purpose, and their regular breaks made them more efficient.

There is no exact science around exactly how long your break should be or precisely how long you work before you break. The key factor is figuring out the pulse-and-pause cycle that works best for you.

Keep in mind that not all breaks are necessarily good ones. Be sure to choose breaks that stave off fatigue, such as engaging in meditation, talking with a friend, setting goals, napping, or doing light exercises like stretching or taking a brisk walk.

An empty vessel has nothing to give; be sure to fill yourself back up before pouring yourself out again.

Principle #4 Summary

- The best way to prevent exhaustion and burnout is to create loving boundaries with respect to our time.
- The same boundaries we institute for those around us, we need to implement for ourselves, ensuring we are getting

the proper amount of sleep and rest so that we can show up as our best, most refreshed and recharged selves.
- Our words are powerful, so be careful with your *yes* and learn how to lovingly say *no*.

Putting Principle #4 Into Practice

1. On a scale of 1 to 10 (1 being the least, 10 being the most), how stressed do you feel on a daily, weekly basis? Can you identify the source of your stress?
2. Outside of work, what life events or responsibilities cause you the most stress? How can you better manage your stress?
3. Are you happy and fulfilled in your current job situation? If not, why not? What type of work would be most fulfilling to you?
4. How easy is it for you to say 'no' on a scale of 1 to 10 (1 being the hardest, 10 being the easiest)?
5. Are you in the habit of saying yes to people, and not following through? If so, why do you think you do this? How can you improve in this area?
6. How are you with respect to taking time for rest and self-care (1 being the worst, 10 being the best)? What are some ways you can implement self-care into your daily, weekly routines?
7. How many hours of sleep do you get per night?
8. Do you make time in your day to take breaks? If not, why not? If so, how has this helped your mental, physical and spiritual health?

Challenge: Create a time in your day to rest. This could be a nap, a time of not working, doing something that rejuvenates and invigorates.

PRINCIPLE #5: USING YOUR TIME AS CURRENCY

"The key is in not spending time, but in investing it."

— STEPHEN R. COVEY

As we opened in the introduction to this book, we addressed the fact that we all have the same 24 hours within a day. We also discussed how time, like money, is used however we see fit, on what is important to us, what we value. Money buys goods and experiences, and if we have enough money, it can actually give us more freedom of time.

The way we use our time could be the difference in whether we are broke or wealthy. When we procrastinate and waste our time, we pass up opportunities for growth and goal achievement. When we are good stewards of our time, we expand our possibilities for accomplishments, experiences, and connection with others.

The truth remains that none of us can actually add a single hour to our day, or a year to our life, and for this reason, time is the great equalizer. In this section, we will look at time as a currency, how we can spend, save, invest and distribute it.

TIME CONSUMPTION

As humans, we are consumers of many things - food, drinks, sports, entertainment, and the like. In general, the term "time consumption" often holds a negative connotation, referring to activities that waste our time. While this widely known use of the word may be true, there are also ways in which we can consume time in a positive manner. For instance, hobbies, serving others, working, passion projects, and spending time with friends and family are all great causes that consume our time.

TIME IS OUR GREATEST ASSET

Have you ever lost a $100 bill? Ouch, that hurts! My mother has told me on numerous occasions how, in the early 1980s she once lost a $100 bill. At that time $100 was worth much more than it is today. However, even with the depreciation of the dollar, I don't know too many people who would be alright with losing that amount of money.

What could you do with $100 today? For starters, you could have a really long receipt at the dollar store. You could buy a couple of pairs of shoes, a decent seat at a concert, a solo trip to Disneyland, a couple of bags of groceries, a couple of pairs of jeans, or have a fancy meal with a friend.

What if you lost 100 minutes? While you can earn another $100, you can never earn back 100 lost minutes. We know that there will never be the same day on the calendar repeated, ever. So why is it so much easier for us to throw away time than money?

Time is an asset, and with any asset, it is something that must be cherished, protected, and ultimately used wisely. I have heard too many people say, "Where did the time go?" and "If there were just more hours in a day." If there were more hours in a day, then what? Basically, they are saying if there were more hours in a day, they would be more productive. Time used as an asset equals productivity, and time used haphazardly equals ineffectiveness. Just like you would not throw a $100 bill out of your car window, stop throwing your time away because you will never be able to gain it back.

TIME IS MONEY

"Time is money," a phrase that often makes me think of a busy office, and an overbearing boss standing on a desk screaming, from a megaphone, "Faster people, time is money!"

It certainly takes time to make money, and if you work at an hourly rate or even on a yearly salary, this will absolutely be felt. In these cases, time has a direct effect on money. Some people call this trading time for money. Yet, this principle is not only to be applied to the workforce.

Let's take a vacation for example. The more time you spend in that wonderfully relaxing destination or toe-curling adventure, the more money it will cost to be there. Or have you ever been late on a credit card bill? That tardiness just cost you a fee.

On a more abstract level, the time we spend making plans, making deals, making follow-up calls to clients, or finishing a project, or the converse, can have a direct effect on our bank account.

In all these cases, elapsed time has either a direct or indirect effect on our money.

BUYING TIME

We discussed in Chapter 10, Time Management 101, the importance of delegating certain tasks, so you truly focus on your genius, which is often tied to the ability to make an income.

When we are bogged down with the mundane, but necessary tasks of life, this takes away from focusing on what's most important to us, our gifts to the world, spending more time with loved ones, and even making more money. As Jack Canfield and Rachel Rodgers discuss in their books, *Success Principles* and *We Should All be Millionaires*, respectively, it is not a matter of being above these types of activities, but rather choosing how to best utilize our time.

I'm confident that I could learn to make my own clothes, change my own car oil, or do my own taxes. However, since none of these actually interest me, nor am I skilled at, I would much rather pay someone who is, so I do not have to use my time. The beautiful thing about life, and people, is that we all have our specific gifts, talents, and abilities. My passions include writing, planning and strategizing, interior decorating, running businesses, performing arts, and serving people. It is in these areas that I choose to focus my time. So when my sink clogs up, instead of pulling out a manual on how to fix it, I call a plumber. In essence, I bought and paid for time, and of course, a sink that works.

INVESTING TIME

The word *invest (verb)*, defined by Merriam-Webster, means to commit (money) in order to earn a financial return, or to make use of for future benefits or advantages. It can also mean to involve or engage emotionally.

We invest in stocks, real estate, and in businesses. The key to investments is that it is about creating a future return, which means it does not happen in an instant, but rather takes time to mature before we can actually see a profit.

Nothing worth having in this life happens without effort; thus, in order to invest in ourselves, our families, friends, and our futures, we need to make a concerted effort and devote a significant amount of time.

There are many ways in which we can invest in ourselves and those around us. Perhaps it is taking a course so as to build your skillset for the future of your career. We can invest in others by mentoring or being mentored. Taking a vacation is an investment in your mental health. Setting aside time to pray and meditate is an investment in our spiritual well-being. Getting a massage or having a regularly scheduled workout routine is an investment in our physical health, while starting a business venture is an attempt to invest in our future financial security. Investing time in our family and friends strengthens bonds, which is good for our emotional health.

What are some ways you can decide to invest in yourself or those you love?

SPENDING TIME

Earlier, we discussed how, unlike money, you can never gain back your time. With a commodity so precious, fleeting, and fragile, shouldn't we guard it, cherish, and spend it wisely? Why do you think so many people desire to be wealthy? Is it only for the ability to buy things and take fancy vacations? I imagine that is part of it, but what money truly does is gives us the freedom to spend our *time* the way we choose.

It is clear that we can spend our time on what we choose, but only some activities actually yield a solid return on investment (ROI). For example, if you watch television for an hour, you've spent one hour on that activity. Unless you learned something from the show, other than being entertained, you did not really gain or achieve anything. On the other hand, if you spent one hour working on a home improvement or passion project, you still spent that time, yet you received an ROI because that hour got you closer to a goal.

Note: I think I have made it clear throughout the course of this book that I am in no way condemning having fun, watching television or any number of non-productive activities. However, when we are looking from a productivity lens, then we need to be careful to make concerted efforts to dedicate a significant amount of time on the activities whereby we reap the greatest return on our time investment.

BUDGETING TIME

We're all familiar with the concept of creating a budget for our income and expenses. We know how much money we make per month, and we know what we have left to play with after all the bills and financial obligations are taken care of. What if we created a ***Weekly Time Budget*** (See table below and Appendix for blank version).

It could look something like this - A week has 168 hours in it (24 hours x 7 days = gross time income). Let's say you sleep 7 hours a night - good for you! This gives you 119 awake hours per week (net time income). If you work a nine-to-five job, you know that Monday through Friday, you spend 40 hours (expenses), not including commuting. Then you would break down how many hours you have remaining, after work/commute, including nights and weekends. From there, you would subtract any other obligations (expenses), and whatever is left is what you have to play with (surplus). Once you have the whole number, then you can decide exactly how you will spend it. Whether it is time resting or recreating or reaching your goals, it is all yours!

(Sample)Weekly Time Budget		
Daily Activity	**Daily Hrs Spent on Activity**	**Weekly Hrs Spent on Activity (Daily hrs x 7)**
	Total Weekly Hours = 24 hrs/day x 7 days/week = 168 hrs/week	
Work	8	56
Commute	1	7
Cooking	2	14
Workout	1.5	10.5
Kids activities/homework	2	14
Sleep	7.5	52.5
	Total Weekly Hrs Spent - Add up all numbers in the "Weekly Hrs Spent on Activity" column	154
	Total Weekly Hrs Remaining (Surplus) - Subtract above total from total weekly hours (168) for total surplus hours remaining	14

SAVING TIME

Have you ever heard your GPS say, "You can save 5 minutes if you choose this route?" and you gladly hit the "Yes" or "Continue on new route" button. Who doesn't like to save time? What would you do if you had an extra hour each day, a time in which you could do whatever you pleased? Just like saving a few dollars because of a well-redeemed coupon, we like to save our time. Of course, you can't put it in the bank, earn interest, or use it at a later date, but within the day or moment, it is a wonderful thing. For a detailed list of time savers, re-read Chapter 12 - *Shrinking & Growing Time*, in the section on "Maximizing your time."

GIVING TIME

There have been numerous studies on how giving back to society and serving others helps with our mindset, psyche, overall mood, and feelings of fulfillment in this life. When we take the time to give to others in need, it helps us to become more grateful. Gratitude creates a healthy mindset, and it's been proven time and again that a healthy mind is imperative for overall health. If you've ever volunteered your time, you know that it is virtually impossible to walk away feeling grumpy. In fact, it is more likely that you will leave with a greater sense of fulfillment than when you arrived. My philosophy about volunteering is to choose something that resonates with you and your values. For instance, if you love the outdoors, you might consider participating in an outdoor service project, such as a beach cleanup, trail building, or park maintenance. If you love children, maybe you could choose to be a mentor or tutor. Love art? Volunteer at an arts agency, mural or beautification project.

There are many ways you can find volunteer opportunities in your area, and one of my favorite sites is www.idealist.org. If you choose a different search source, most, if not all, nonprofit organizations have opportunities for involvement. Simply look at their website under the section about getting involved. I can guarantee you, volunteering will never be a waste of time, and you will walk away changed, challenged, and elevated.

Principle #5 Summary

- Time is a currency, and while you cannot actually, physically take it to the bank, it has an indirect effect on our money.
- Unlike money, time can never be replaced. With this knowledge, we should view time as even more precious than money, cherishing it, valuing it, saving it, and using it for the most important things and people in our lives.

Putting Principle #5 Into Practice

1. If you believed that 100 hours was the same as $100 how would this shift the way you utilize your time?
2. What are ways you can save time in your current daily, weekly regimen?
3. What are some ways you can give of your time?
4. In what area(s) of your life do you tend to make the most investments of time?

Challenge: Create a time budget, and stick to it for one month.

CONCLUSION

Life is short, short, short. Even if you live to be 100 years old, in comparison with the generations of people who have walked the earth, the mountains, the oceans, and the deserts, which took billions of years to form, we have a limited time here. Each day you receive a new paycheck equaling 24, not dollars, but hours.

Whether you are a stay-at-home parent, business mogul, super mega star, time is the great equalizer, for no one has more or fewer hours in a day than the next person. How will you choose to spend, save, relish and cherish the hours that are daily gifted to you?

If you break down your life in sections of 10-20 years, your life may look a little something like this. Age 0-20 - growth, development, school, and living in the confines of your parents' rules. Ages 20-30 (if you went to college), you would have likely graduated and secured your first, second, or third job out of college. If you skipped college, perhaps you are honing your skills in your trade, skill or profession. Between 30-40, depending on where you live, you will likely have been married, have had a couple of children, and maybe bought a home (depending upon how much school debt you have).

Now, 40-50, your young children are tweens, teens or even young adults. If you own a home, you have started to see some good equity, you have settled into your career, or you have changed careers by this point, at least once. Maybe you've taken some trips outside of the country, and you are starting to think about retirement a little more. At 50-60, your kids are out of the house, hallelujah! Or you're super sad about this. You are starting to think about when you will retire, and what you will do with yourself once you do. Now at 60-70, retirement is so close, and you can't wait to take that cruise around the world, downsize your home, and spend time with your grandkids.

If you are fortunate enough to make it to 80, you will have lived for a total of 700,800 24-hour days over the span of your life. If you're 20, 80 years may seem like a long way away, but take it from me, it goes fast, and the older we become, the clock, for whatever reason, seems to speed up.

My hope is that I fulfill my life's mission/purpose during the short amount of time I have here on this planet. My hope is that I leave my little corner of the world better than I found it, and that people can look back on my life with fondness, joy, and gratitude for the mark I left upon their hearts and souls.

So the big question is this: with the limited time you have here on this planet, what do you want to accomplish? How do you want to be remembered? What legacy do you want to leave for your children, grandchildren, nieces, nephews and the world?

Will you use your time living in regret, fear, or frustration over the battles that you cannot win or the people you cannot change, or will you use it in gratitude, pursuing joy, loving those around you, and finding what it is you were put here to do? How will you spend your 24-hour currency?

REFERENCES

- (1997). What is the function of the various brainwaves? Scientific American. <https://www.scientificamerican.com/article/what-is-the-function-of-t-1997-12-22/> (2020 October, 20).
- (2020). The Science of Deep Breathing and Why It's Vital to Health. Clarity Clinic. <https://www.claritychi.com/the-science-of-deep-breathing-and-why-its-vital-to-health/> (2025, January 21).
- (2017). Are Shorter Working Days The Secret To A Happier, Healthier And More Productive Life? You Matter. <https://youmatter.world/en/schedules-working-days-productivity/#:~:text=As%20well%2C%20there%20are%20also,more%20concentrated%20in%20the%20morning> (2021, May 6).
- (2018). Take a Break: Why Rest is the Foundation of Physical Health. Advent Health. <https://www.adventhealth.com/hospital/adventhealth-tampa/blog/take-a-break-why-rest-foundation-physical-health> (2024, June 10).
- (2019). The science behind morning people and night owls. Urban. <https://urban.co/editorial/science-behind-morning-people-night-owls/> (2021, July 6).
- (2025). Dictionary.com. <https://www.dictionary.com/browse/regret> (2024, June 11).
- (2025). Merriam Webster. <https://www.merriam-webster.com/dictionary/invest> (2025, January 21).
- Allen, David. *Getting Things Done: The Art of Stressfree Productivity*. Penguin Books, 2001.
- Andre, C. (2019). Proper Breathing Brings Better Health. Scientific American. <https://www.scientificamerican.com/article/proper-breathing-brings-better-health/> (2025, January 21).
- Ang, B. (2016). Calling it a day at 3.30pm: Firms help employees strike work-life balance. The Straits Times. <https://www.straitstimes.com/lifestyle/calling-it-a-day-at-330pm-firms-help-employees-strike-work-life-balance> (2021, May 6 May).
- Agnvall, E. (2014). Stress! Don't Let It Make You Sick. AARP. <https://www.aarp.org/health/healthy-living/info-2014/stress-and-disease.html> (2024, February 5).
- Al-Achrafi, S. (2017). Theta - Entering the World of Our Subconscious. Huffpost. <https://www.huffpost.com/entry/theta-entering-the-world-of-our-subconscious_b_59a19597e4b0d0ef9f1c1452#:~:text=Theta%

20brain%20waves%2C%20measured%20at,conscious%20and%20the%20subconscious%20worlds.&text=While%20in%20a%20theta%20state,profound%20learning%2C%20healing%20and%20growth> (2020, October 20).

- Becker, J. The Lost Practice of Resting One Day Each Week. Becoming Minimalist. <https://www.becomingminimalist.com/resting/> (2024, June 10).
- Byron, L. & Brandon, P. (2024). Why Do We Need Sleep? Sleep Foundation. <https://www.sleepfoundation.org/how-sleep-works/why-do-we-need-sleep> (2024, June 3).
- Canfield, Jack & Switzer, Janet. *The Success Principles: How to Get from Where you are to Where you Want to Be.* Collins, 2006.
- Cherry, K. (2023). What Your Favorite Season Says About Your Personality. Very Well Mind. <https://www.verywellmind.com/what-your-favorite-season-say-about-personality-4114006> (2020, November 7).
- Cherry, K. (2025). How Multitasking Affects Productivity and Brain Health. Very Well Mind. <https://www.verywellmind.com/multitasking-2795003> (2024, July 8).
- Covey, Stephen. R. *The 7 Habits of Highly Effective People.* Free Press, 1989.
- Diffley, J. 5 Reasons Why You Need To Recharge. Select Health. <https://selecthealth.org/blog/2018/04/5-reasons-why-you-need-to-recharge-on-a-regular-basis> (2024, April 4).
- Eske. J. (2019). The effects of going more than 24 hours without sleep. Medical News Today. <https://www.medicalnewstoday.com/articles/324799> (2024, March 6).
- Eldredge, John. *Waking the Dead: The Glory of a Heart Fully Alive.* Thomas Nelson, 2003.
- Fact Checked. (2024). How Long Can You Go Without Sleep? Nectar. <https://www.nectarsleep.com/posts/how-long-can-you-go-without-sleep/> (2024, June 3). Goldberg, J. MD. (2014). 10 Health Problems Related to Stress That You Can Fix. WebMD. <https://www.webmd.com/balance/stress-management/features/10-fixable-stress-related-health-problems> (2020, September 5).
- Fran (2022). 5 top tips on how to avoid procrastination. Future Learn. <https://www.futurelearn.com/info/blog/stop-procrastinating-top-tips> (2024, September 6).
- Greenfield, R. (2016). The six-hour work day increases productivity. So will Britain and America adopt one? Independent. <https://www.independent.co.uk/news/business/six-hour-work-day-increases-productivity-so-will-britain-and-america-adopt-one-sweden-a7066961.html> (2021, May 6).

- Griffiths, G. The Science Behind Procrastination. ATC UNSW Student life. <https://www.arc.unsw.edu.au/blitz/read/The-Science-Behind-Procrastination> (2021, April 15).
- Gupta, A. (2022). Slow down and practice 'waking rest' to keep stress at bay throughout the day. Health Shots. <https://www.healthshots.com/mind/happiness-hacks/here-are-the-benefits-of-rest-and-doing-nothing/> (2024, June 10).
- How Long Does It Take a Train to Stop? Minnesota Operation Lifesaver. <https://www.minnesotasafetycouncil.org/ol/stop.cfm#:~:text=The%20average%20freight%20train%20is,about%20a%20mile%20to%20stop> (2020, Sept 3).
- How Long Should a Nap Be? (2020). Sleep Score Labs. <https://www.sleepscore.com/blog/how-long-should-i-nap/> (2024, June 3).
- Jackson, E. (2012)The 25 Biggest Regrets In Life. What Are Yours? Forbes. <https://www.forbes.com/sites/ericjackson/2012/10/18/the-25-biggest-regrets-in-life-what-are-yours/#740775e76488> (2023, November 5).
- Jaffe, E. (2015). Morning People Vs. Night Owls: 9 Insights Backed by Science. Fast Company. <https://www.fastcompany.com/3046391/morning-people-vs-night-people-9-insights-backed-by-science> (2021, July 6).
- Jansen, E. (2020). Sleep 101: Why Sleep Is So Important to Your Health. Michigan State: School of Public Health. <https://sph.umich.edu/pursuit/2020posts/why-sleep-is-so-important-to-your-health.html> (2024, June 3).
- Katsos, T. (2021). Brainwaves & Consciousness: Understanding Brainwave Frequencies. Mind your Reality. <https://www.mind-your-reality.com/brain_waves.html> (2020, October 20).
- Korhonen, V. (2024). Life expectancy in North America 2022. Statista. <https://www.statista.com/statistics/274513/life-expectancy-in-north-america/> (2024, January 12).
- Lewis, T. (2016). This One Factor May Explain Why You're a Morning Person or a Night Owl. Science Alert. <https://www.sciencealert.com/this-one-factor-may-explain-why-you-re-a-morning-person-or-a-night-owl> (2020, July 6).
- Mayo Clinic Staff. (2024). Napping: Do's and don'ts for healthy adults. Mayo Clinic. <https://www.mayoclinic.org/healthy-lifestyle/adult-health/in-depth/napping/art-20048319#:~:text=Keep%20naps%20short.,are%20to%20feel%20groggy%20afterward> (2024, June 3).
- Mele, C. (2016). Paper Calendars Endure Despite the Digital Age. The New York Times. <https://www.nytimes.com/2016/12/29/business/paper-calendars.html> (2021, August 12).

- Merle, A. (2019). How To Hack Into The Alpha Brain Wave State. Medium. <https://medium.com/@andrewmerle/how-to-hack-into-the-alpha-brain-wave-state-20508f81b7e0> (2020, October 20).
- Mindfulness. Psychology Today. <https://www.psychologytoday.com/us/basics/mindfulness> (2025, January 15).
- Miller, J. (2018). Self-Compassion as the Heart of Self-Care. The New Social Worker. <https://www.socialworker.com/feature-articles/self-care/self-compassion-heart-of-self-care/#:~:text=Self%2Dcompassion%20is%20generally%20defined,kind%20and%20considerate%20to%20oneself> (2024, April 4).
- Milner, C. & Cote, K. (2009). Benefits of napping in healthy adults: impact of nap length, time of day, age, and experience with napping. National Library of Medicine. <https://pubmed.ncbi.nlm.nih.gov/19645971/> (2024, June 3).
- Moran, Brian P. & Lennington, Michael. *The 12 Week Year: Get More Done in 12 Weeks Than Others do in 12 Months.* Wiley, 2013.
- Newton's First Law. The Physics Classroom. <https://www.physicsclassroom.com/class/newtlaws/Lesson-1/Newton-s-First-Law> (2020, December 5).
- Pak, E. (2020). Walt Disney's Rocky Road to Success. Biography. <https://www.biography.com/news/walt-disney-failures> (2021, April 12).
- Power, R. (2017). A Day of Rest: 12 Scientific Reasons It Works. Inc. <https://www.inc.com/rhett-power/a-day-of-rest-12-scientific-reasons-it-works.html> (2024, June 10).
- Roberts, L. (2010). Short breaks make people happier than one long holiday, psychologists claim. The Telegraph. <https://www.telegraph.co.uk/travel/travelnews/7946668/Short-breaks-make-people-happier-than-one-long-holiday-psychologists-claim.html> (2021, May 6).
- Rodgers, Rachel. *We Should All Be Millionaires: A Woman's Guide to Earning More, Building Wealth, and Gaining Economic Power.* Harper Collins, 2021.
- Rodrigues, F.R. (2022). Creative workout of the week: How to avoid burnout syndrome in you workspace. Nomadx Foundation. <https://nomadx.foundation/blog/creative-workout-of-the-week-how-to-avoid-burnout-syndrome-in-you-workspace?> (2024, August 2).
- Rubin, G. (2013). Are You a Tortoise or a Hare? About Work. Psychology Today. <https://www.psychologytoday.com/us/blog/the-happiness-project/201304/are-you-tortoise-or-hare-about-work> (2021, April 12).
- Saplakoglu, Y. (2019). Night Owls and Morning Larks, Make Room for Afternoon People and Nappers. Live Science. <https://www.livescience.com/65688-afternoon-person-nappers-chronotypes.html> (2020, Dec 10).

- Scott, B. (2020). How to practice self-care through self-compassion. Scrubbing In. <https://scrubbing.in/how-to-practice-self-care-through-self-compassion/> (2024, April 4).
- Staff Writer (2015). What Percentage of Our Lives Are Spent Working? Reference. <https://www.reference.com/world-view/percentage-lives-spent-working-599e3f7fb2c88fca> (2020, March 20).
- Suni, E. & Rosen, D. (2024). Mastering Sleep Hygiene: Your Path to Quality Sleep. Sleep Foundation. <https://www.sleepfoundation.org/sleep-hygiene> (2024, June 3).
- Terkeurst, Lysa. *Good Boundaries and Goodbyes: Loving Others Without Losing the Best of Who You Are.* Thomas Nelson, 2022.
- Travers, M. (2024). A Psychologist Explains The Power Of 'Vision Boarding' For Success. Forbes. <https://www.forbes.com/sites/traversmark/2024/03/29/a-psychologist-explains-the-power-of-vision-boarding-for-success/> (2025, Feb 11).
- Vozz, S. (2017). This is how Many Minutes of Breaks you Need Each Day. Fast Company. <https://www.fastcompany.com/40487419/this-is-how-many-minutes-of-breaks-you-need-each-day> (2025, January 21).
- Voyager, V. (2020). From Procrastination to Motivation: Manipulating Dopamine. Medium. <https://medium.com/age-of-awareness/from-pro crastination-to-motivation-manipulating-dopamine-9c1a345b9bda> (2020, March 2).
- What is the Definition of Futuristic. Gallup. <https://www.gallup.com/cliftonstrengths/en/252248/futuristic-theme.aspx> (2021, June 3)
- Why is Sleep Important? (2022). NIH. <https://www.nhlbi.nih.gov/health/sleep/why-sleep-important#:~:text=During%20sleep%2C%20your%20body%20is,long%2Dterm)%20health%20problems> (2024, June 3).
- Wilkinson, Bruce. *The Dream Giver.* Multnomah, 1984.

www.ingramcontent.com/pod-product-compliance
Lightning Source LLC
LaVergne TN
LVHW010653110826
845149LV00014B/3060

* 9 7 9 8 9 9 3 1 7 4 8 0 8 *